Praise for *Smashi*

ig

One thing that Sandra Westla _eiling_ is not, is another text bewailing the inequa~~ny~~ ~~or~~ ~~p~~ ~~.essional~~ women and their continuing inability to achieve the things that so many deserve. Sandra's book is much more positive, inspiring and practical, as well as being somewhat unique in its approach. Far from being yet another self-help book, this one really opens up the world of possibility for women who for reasons known only to themselves, have constructed their own personal glass ceilings and live their lives believing they are unable to change.

Using NLP techniques, guided imagery work and with a smattering of existential philosophy thrown in together with additional bonuses, Sandra enables women to discover their own uniqueness, to begin to own their passions and to question the values, beliefs and prejudices that have held them back for so long. The change process, which takes place as each activity is undertaken, can only make a positive difference to their future.

Eminently qualified to write such a text, Sandra comes from an education background and herself is an expert therapist and hugely successful woman. Her openness and sharing of her own journey throughout the book inspires the reader, and enables us to realise that this is a programme that has been lived and developed through the process of enquiry, and a questioning of motives, needs, and wants in life before taking that leap of faith to achieve. It is one that has credibility and therefore offers a more honest and real approach to empower the reader to move forward to live extraordinarily.

This book is a must-read for women from all walks of life who have ever questioned their meanings in life, and have craved for the help to make changes for the better. It's here in one book: all the tools you need to smash the glass ceiling and reach your true potential!

Tina Tilmouth, *Author, Teacher and Therapist – Powys*

Sandra has beautifully crafted a truly inspirational book which is a must-read for women everywhere. Irrespective of your background, history or your current positioning on the employment ladder, Sandra will be by your side every step of the way guiding you through the principals of change so you can smash your glass ceiling.

This book will challenge you to your core by confronting long held negative beliefs, your anxieties, what you value, how it is to be you as a woman here and now in the present and how these are contributing to holding you back from what you ultimately desire.

This book will take you on an emotional ride placing your head above your ceiling, to look at all you can be and what you can achieve. Value this book and keep it by your side, refer to it whenever you need, keep that fire inside you burning.

This is the book every woman who wants to succeed has been longing for, written by an amazing woman who I sincerely admire, who challenges my thinking, inspires me and who I model. It is rare in life you find someone that impacts you like this incredible woman has.

So stop making excuses, dare yourself to dream. There is only forwards now; empower yourself to make those dreams a reality. I am.

Teresa Woods, *Account Underwriter – Suffolk*

This book provides an excellent guide for women who wish to look honestly at themselves, assess where they are currently and then move forwards. A major attribute of this book is its accessibility to a range of readers. The language is clear, and explanations of complex processes are concise and described in jargon-free terms. The conversational tone is welcoming and inclusive, and the author's sharing of her own story as an illustration of certain ideas is inspirational.

The reader is taken on a journey of self-discovery, helped all the way by the easy-to-follow step-by-step approach which is clearly explained at the beginning. This and the exercises encourage the reader to stay with it to complete what is a fascinating and revealing experience and, as Sandra says, "an internal revolution." The questions posed are challenging and thought provoking, the exercises likewise.

In these days when, sadly, women are still underrepresented in so many fields and particularly at higher levels in almost all walks of life, this book should prove invaluable. For women who are striving to break through that glass ceiling and fulfil their potential, this book provides a clear, practical and accessible text – a guide to help them to see and, most importantly, achieve their aim and to become who they want to be.

Tina Davies, *Educator – Suffolk*

Sandra has provided a well informed and intriguing exploration of what holds us back as women. I related to many of her well-presented theories and personal examples of thoughts, feelings and behaviours that limit our professional and personal growth. Once you begin to recognise these familiar patterns, it's easy to become captivated by her personable writing style, to uncover solutions and strategies that promote a compelling desire to change. This is a motivating and uplifting guide to exploration of the inner self and what it means to be a professional woman. She explores the familiar territory of Neuro-Linguistic Programming in a unique and specific way that's refreshing and easily understood, with exercises that challenge and stretch your imagination and ambition, smashing and reaching far beyond our glass ceiling. I'm sure this book as part of her Ultimate Programme will inspire, inform and motivate women to greater success for many years to come!

Joan Clark, *RGN, Dip Hyp, NLPP – Essex*

This book takes you on an incredible journey of self-discovery. As an ex-business director, I wish this had been written ten years ago as it really does clarify in a clear and practical way each step to take to really help you get to the top!

Karen Francis, *Mind and Behavioural Expert – Surrey*

SMASHING YOUR GLASS CEILING

8 STEPS TO FREE YOURSELF
AND BE YOURSELF

SANDRA WESTLAND, B.Ed. (Hons), M.A.

PUBLISHING

Acknowledgments

Writing this book, for me, has been quite some amazing journey.

Combining my own life and learning's, my passion to enhance the lives of other women, *and* describing techniques that can tap into the power and potential of the mind into one book has been quite an extraordinary task.

Yet, I couldn't have done it alone. I would like to extend my heartfelt thanks to Raymond Aaron and his incredibly powerful author programme. Raymond's Programme has taken a desire to write a book like this for women to the reality of completing it. An intrinsic part of the success of this project has been due to my personal book architect Lori Murphy, whose support has continually spurred me on. My thanks also go to Marie Littlewort for her inspirational artistic skill in designing the book cover. I would also like to thank Lewis Knights for his superb astuteness for technical and grammatical accuracy.

Writing a book about women becoming all they can be felt overwhelming at first and needed someone wiser than I to get me thinking! So I would also like to thank Tina Davies for her input right at the start, as I formulated and outlined the chapters and their content. She knows so much about being a woman, and about being a wise woman at that. I thank her for all the stands she has made in her life so far for women, and for her enthusiasm in my ideas.

This support has been crucial, but without the constant passion and belief in this project from another, the chance to discuss men, women and business along the way, this project would have been a very different process and would likely have had a very different outcome. For this, I owe a big thank you to Tom Barber. His wealth of knowledge, his patience and his ability to convey unwavering faith and support in writing this book for women has been gratefully received and valued. Thanks, Tom!

I would also like to thank the support that my good friends continue to give me. Yet again, they cheer and spur me on. So Mandy, Sue, Linzie, Tash, Helen, Liz, Sandy and Kirsten, thank you for being in my life. I am very lucky to have such genuine, supportive and caring people around me.

Lastly, I owe a debt of gratitude to all of my clients who have taught me so much about being human, and my past and current students whom I have been fortunate enough to teach and whose enthusiasm and passion for learning inspired me to attempt to write a book such as this.

This book is dedicated to my long standing friends: Mandy, Sue, Linzie, Tash, Helen, Liz, Sandy and Kirsten for without them all, I would not be here as I am today. There is nothing on this earth more to be valued than true friendship.

Contents

Table of Workouts

Throughout this book, there are tasks and exercises to help you explore yourself and also to begin the journey of your inner change. Think of them as mental workouts. They are listed below so you can easily refer to them at any time. I hope you will.

Foreword

Smashing Your Glass Ceiling: 8 Steps to Free Yourself and Be Yourself by Sandra Westland is intended to help you become inspired as a woman, fully knowing that you are extraordinary and can achieve success if you open up to your uniqueness and fully understand the depths you have within.

In exploring and uncovering you and how you are in the world through a variety of techniques and exercises and aligning yourself to just what you are really about, your vision can become truly alive and your ceiling smashed.

This book will get you desiring to move forwards in your life, encourage you to challenge your beliefs, understand your values, find your passions and guide your life into the future of extraordinary success, ultimately learning to be all that you can be.

In this book:

- You will creatively ignite the inner change process.
- You will get to know your unconscious prejudices about women and men and how you really feel being a woman.
- You will discover your unique inner world and how the alignment of yourself at all levels is the key to success.
- You will connect with your inner passions, unite with your potential and know that in formulating your future within, you can easily and naturally make things happen.
- You will learn the power of your mind and just how to use it for immediate changes when things don't go to plan.
- You will smash the glass that is preventing you from the success you deserve.

You owe it to yourself to give this unique programme the chance to make a difference to your life and to smash your glass ceiling. Why not become one of the many people who have completed this programme with Sandra and who have reaped the benefits of exploring themselves in this way to become successful women?

Raymond Aaron
New York Times **Bestselling Author**
www.MillionaireBusinessBootCamp.com

Chapter 1
Let's Hit the Ground Running
How tough does it need to be?

*Would you tell me, please, which way
I ought to go from here?
That depends a good deal on where you
want to get to.
I don't much care where.
Then it doesn't matter which way you go.*
~ Lewis Carroll, *Alice in Wonderland* ~

You have to start somewhere. We all do. I did.

I sat in my school office; it had been a busy start to the day. A school assembly to deliver, a few students to check in with, some letters to write, and a parents' evening to organise for the following week. There were three weeks left: fifteen days, or sixty lessons to teach before the Christmas holidays. Was that really the way to be thinking about my job, the number of lessons left to teach before a holiday? This was my thirteenth year in education, and that day I sat at my desk, looking around at the pile of marking left to do and the one hundred and fifty student reports that were needing to be checked and collated.

I was thirty-four years old, with another twenty-six more years left before retirement. Should I *really* be thinking like this? It didn't feel right. I was wishing my life away. I sat for a while longer, ignoring the papers in front of me, and tried to imagine twenty-six more years of this. That felt seriously depressing. I tried to imagine twenty-six years of something else, anything else. Nothing came to mind! That felt seriously shocking! *So that's that, then*, I thought. *At least I will get a good pension at the end of this stretch.*

I sat a few moments more, shaken by how I couldn't imagine what else I could do in life. *Pathetic*, I said to myself, pushing the chair back, standing up and making my way out of the door and towards the sports hall, and the badminton lesson I was going to next teach. But that day was my start; something was set in motion. An internal revolution had begun. "Just what *can* you do?" "Just what *are* you capable of?" was murmuring away and beginning to ignite something within me. And so I made a start. Those questions have never gone away.

It's never too late – never too late to start over,
never too late to be happy.
~ Jane Fonda ~

Does your past have power over you? Are you constantly being reminded of the last time you felt embarrassed, or didn't reach a target? Does your behaviour try to help you avoid what happened previously when things didn't go to plan? Do you live totally in the present, consumed by it even, trying to manage what needs to be done right now, forgetting what you did yesterday and blinded as to the time you have tomorrow, constantly feeling like you're in crisis, with never enough time? Well, you're not alone. This is exactly where I was at until I began to feel unrest within and ask some questions of myself.

So many of the women I've worked with, both personally and on my workshops, have begun questioning themselves and their life in this way. Many of them not just trapped in the now or the past, but fixated on the future and about meeting their next target at all costs.

There are two questions I want you to consider right here and now:

Are you ready to do something about it? And will you do everything in your means to fulfil your dreams? If your answers are yes, then I'm overjoyed that you've decided to read this book, as this is a very real possibility.

> Your vision will become clear only when you
> can look into your own heart.
> Who looks outside, dreams; who looks inside, awakes.
> **~ Carl Jung ~**

This book is about grabbing hold of your life and taking control of your journey through it. Make no mistake: time isn't bothered about excuses; it will pass on by anyway, without you if need be. Why not be a part of *your* time and enjoy becoming the you that you deserve, where you are feeling and being successful?

This programme will empower you as a woman to be successful in both life and in business, whether rising up the ranks of your company or becoming the owner of your own business, it doesn't matter. I want to get you thinking about yourself in a very different way, to uncover your inner resources, and to propel you towards your possibilities.

Some people I know think there is a need for radical changes to be made, a thought which stops them in their tracks from even beginning such a journey. This journey, however, will be much more subtle and much more profound, as it's about letting go of the frustration of *trying* to change things in your life, and opening yourself up to a questioning and a sense of curiosity about things in your life, and in you, and in this process, letting a natural change unfold.

Now is the time to stand still for a moment and focus on the road ahead, the road that is full of possibilities, potentials and passions.

Now is the time to stop looking through your rear view mirror or living life facing where you have come from. It's time to start going somewhere, and really looking at where that somewhere is. Are you ready? Good! Let's begin with something you do every day ... imagining. I have a visualisation I want you to experience, to start the ball rolling as quickly as possible.

This journey you are beginning asks you to explore the powerful mind state of curiosity, so start to allow yourself to become curious as to how your mind responds and what it presents to you from this moment on. Everything you will learn will be important here, because your reactions to what you will encounter and experience in this book and to the images created by your mind in response to them are significant, as they are all clues as to what's going on for you, and, more importantly, what will help you be all you want to be.

I cannot remember the number of times I have heard the people I work with at this point say, "But I can't visualise," or "I just don't have any imagination." This is simply your current understanding of the power of your mind. It's actually very helpful, as it shows us immediately what may be influencing you, and why success just isn't happening for you right now. The more creative and imaginative you can learn to become, the greater the opportunities you will notice, amazingly create, and hungrily move towards. You'll become inventive and flexible, more effective at communicating and solving problems, and you will open yourself up to really experiencing the possibilities of your life. So, you need to get creative and imaginative. It's a prerequisite!

Milton Erickson (1901 – 1980) was a world-famous therapist, known for his ingeniously creative use of language to help people overcome their difficulties, by unlocking their inner unconscious knowledge. He passionately believed that the individual experiencing the "problem" was the best person to know how to overcome it, so he helped people access their unconscious minds to creatively find the resources they needed to solve the problem. This is what we are going to do in this book, creatively find the inner resources that you already possess, and need to get in touch with.

We all experience our imagination to a greater or lesser degree, and if yours is less creative than you would like it to be, then you're already now on the path to enhancing it. How can you speed things up? How can you fast track your imagination's creativity? Well, to start with, you might try taking yourself to an art gallery, take a different route to work to change the view, watch and experience a ballet, read a different kind of book than you're used to, and listen to music – all kinds of music! Simply do some new things that stimulate your mind that you haven't done before or maybe haven't done in a while. Do something new ... anything! Re-awaken and start nourishing your imagination. It's crucial so that you can unleash the creativity you have within, because that creativity is the very thing that will help you once and for all.

Keep in mind a well-known saying used in the Neuro-Linguistic Programming model, "If you always do what you've always done, you'll always get what you've always got," and make a start at doing something different. How about writing a short story on the train home or sketching something in your lunch break? It doesn't matter if you think you can write a story or draw, or not; just start a new creative habit and get those creative neurons stoked up, and firing electricity!

Action is the foundational key to all success.
~ *Pablo Picasso* ~

If at this very moment you feel you aren't able to visualise, or feel resistant or reluctant to continue, then this is most definitely the time to give it a go. Why? Because there are many things to learn about yourself, and creatively visualising will give you the greatest chance of reaching the depths of your inner world. Imagine opening up to your imagination and creativity and combining it with your logical mind. Just imagine what a force you will be! There you go: you've just imagined! It's easy when you know how and have a reason and purpose, which is another thing we are going to find!

Visualising and imagining doesn't need to be in neat, colourful, clear pictures, like watching a movie or looking at a picture or photograph. Visualising can be experienced through many different sensations, sounds, thoughts, feelings, tastes and smells. In fact, all of these are vital for your mind and body to fully engage and synthesize and for you to fully be in the present, planning the future you really want.

> Imagination is more
> Important than knowledge.
> For while knowledge defines all we
> currently know and understand,
> imagination points to all we might yet
> discover and create.
> **~ Albert Einstein ~**

Here are some tips to start visualising:

1) Be as relaxed as possible before starting. Take about five minutes to guide yourself through a simple relaxation process of slow, steady breathing, followed by taking your body through a complete muscle relaxation experience.

Your First Bonus: Bonus Number 1

Here is my special Bonus Number 1, so that you can make the best possible start. My "Relaxation" MP3 Download is something I give to all those on my Success Programme as it makes focusing much easier. Simply go to www.SandraWestlandMedia.com and you will be able to download your copy absolutely free! Listen, relax and enjoy.

2) As each part of this visualisation is written down, you can take your time and build the image that I direct you to. Stop at any point, contemplate and reflect. Write things down as they occur to you, so that you are cementing what's coming to mind. You're beginning to take part in one of the most powerful change processes ever in your life, so don't rush. You can open and/or close your eyes at any point – whatever is most effective for you – and make a note of the feelings you get and what appears as important or meaningful to you as we go along. This is your chance to explore where your mind, brain and body take you. Remember: everything is important, notable and worthy of observation.

3) Visualise using your preferred sense. What do I mean by this? If you don't feel you are able to "see" the images as if you were looking at a picture, it's likely that your natural method for coding internal experiences and bringing them to mind is through another of your senses like hearing, touch, taste, or smell. We all process differently. Go with what works for you. Test out imagining the visualisations below in these different ways to find what's most prominent for you.

If I ask you to imagine being on a beach, what comes to mind? You might *see* yourself there and notice the clear blue sky, or *feel* the sand between your toes, or the sun on your skin, or you might immediately go to the *sound* of the sea, or of children playing.

If I ask you to visualise money … what happens? Do you imagine rifling through the notes *feeling* them, or *hearing* the sound as you shuffle them, or do you *see* a pile of notes?

Have you ever heard of the saying, "I can smell the money"? Or "I can taste success"?

These are good examples of how we use our senses in our experiencing.

Whichever one strikes you and means something is how you'll visualise in the best way for you. So did you *see* things, *hear* things or *feel* things? There is no right or wrong way, so simply go with how it naturally happens for you. As long as you can imagine an orange, the front of your home or your car, then you can visualise more than well enough; it just may not be as clear as you think it should be. If you fill your basic image with whichever sense brings the image alive (sight, sound, touch, taste or smell), then you really have something to work with.

4) Practice is central for transformation and fundamental to any change process, so get practicing.

Now let's try this visualisation, remembering to use sight, sound, feelings, smells and taste …

Exercise 1: Fork in the Road Visualisation

This is one of the first processes we use on the Success Programme as it quickly gets personal! This visualisation helps you get vividly in touch with making the change choices that are most congruent for you and creates awareness about your responsibility in the process of changing your life. Allow whatever emerges to simply be there, unquestioned and un-judged.

Sit quietly for a while and take yourself through a simple body relaxation by listening to the MP3 download in Bonus 1, and clear your mind. You are about to embark on a fascinating journey of discovery ... where you are, and where you are heading.

Just imagine you are walking along a path. This path represents your journey in life. The path behind you is your past and the path ahead is your future. Note the scenery that comes to light as you walk along the path and become aware of how you're feeling, and what you're thinking as you travel along it.

Write everything down as you go along. If you go to my website (at www.SandraWestlandMedia.com) you can download the *Smashing Your Glass Ceiling Workbook*™ that contains all of the exercises that are within this book with spaces to record your experiences, or you can simply write things down in a journal in a way that fits for you.

The journey starts on the path above. As you walk, you see ahead of you a fork in the path ... As the path divides, one path veers off to your left, whilst the other moves forward and to the right. Just stand for a moment and observe the two paths before you read on.

Now, you can choose to travel down the right road or the left road. I'm not going to tell you which - only you can choose the right road for you.

Before you choose the "right" road for you, let's look at both roads and see what they hold. The road on the left is slightly downhill, so, on this path, you can simply coast your way into your future just as you are now. It is the road of doing what you have been doing thus far in your adult life. It means continuing with everything that you have in your life now in the same way. If you have always felt dissatisfied or disappointed at work, then this will continue as such. If you have always longed to travel, and haven't got round to it, this will always be so on this path. If you have always yearned to write, set up your own business, get fit, or be more assertive ... then travelling down the left path will always mean that you will feel these yearnings. You will always be wishing, hoping and wanting these things. The path is predictable and predetermined and you can see it continues for many miles, as far as you can see into the distance. The slope downwards keeps you moving along this path without any effort at all. In fact it would be hard to stop yourself from going in the direction that the path has laid out for you once on it, due to its inevitable momentum.

Consider now:

> What is this like for you?
> What are you thinking?
> How does this feel?

Now imagine you have been travelling on this path for two years ... So if you continue with your life, as it is right now, for another two years ...

Consider:

> What is it like?
> Are you happy to have had another two years of the same journey?
> Are you pleased with your achievements?
> Are you content with life?
> Do you want to keep going along this path?

Imagine you have been travelling on this same path, for the last five to ten years.

Consider:

> How does it all seem now?
> Is life "good enough?"
> Have you had challenges, personal growth, and enjoyed life thus far?
> Have you done enough, seen enough, been enough?

When I have explored this scenario with clients and on my workshops, it usually emphasizes a lack, a "greyness," a sense of despair. It may have been comfortable enough, but appeared quite dull, empty and mundane. Life was a disappointment, and at times frustrating. Some people have described feeling regret, wondering what could have been, and what may have been possible. I have yet to find anybody that having explored it, wants to take this path - yet if you "do" nothing, this is how life will unfold!

Now, let's return to the fork in the road and on to the right path. You notice the right path goes uphill and downhill, and meanders, so you can see and sense it has a few obstructions along the way that will be challenging, but not impossible to move beyond. It is intriguing, interesting and absorbing. You are free to move in a way that you wish, and you have choices as to how you work with the challenges you encounter along the way. You don't know where you will end up if you follow this path, but it seems not to matter, as the journey along this path is so incredibly fascinating and engaging. You sense that along the way you will really learn more about yourself, what you are capable of and all that you can do in your life. After all, you can only find your limits when tested and pushed, which this path will introduce you to.

So consider now:
> What is this like for you?
> What are you thinking?
> How does this feel?

Now imagine you've been travelling on this path for two years ... So if you continue with your life along this path for another two years ...

Consider:
> What is it like?
> Are you happy to have had another two years of the same?
> Are you pleased with your achievements?
> Are you content with life?
> How different is this to the left path?

Imagine you have been travelling on this same path, for the last five to ten years.

Consider:

> How does it all seem now?
>
> Is life "good enough"?
>
> Have you had challenges, personal growth, and enjoyed life thus far?
>
> Have you done enough, seen enough, been enough?

Upon exploring this with the people I work with, there is usually a visible change in them with the realisations they uncover. An energy that radiates from deep inside them; an opening up to a sense of freedom and a desire to live the life they now see, and learn about what else life has to offer. This path seems to create an inner confidence, contentment and *success awareness*, a sense of experiencing and engaging in life, and all that it can potentially offer. Along this path I find that people realise they have nothing to prove to anyone, that they can simply thrive and learn about being in life and embracing the demands and joys it brings. There is born a sense of resilience, of being able to cope and even thrive off of setbacks and challenges (which no longer seem as such).

As I worked my way up the promotional ladder to senior teacher status, with my sights set on a head teacher position, I worked long hours, devoured mountains of paperwork, was enmeshed in meetings, the next student trauma, and the targets that had to be meet. My journey at that time was most definitely on the left path. I was working hard with no time for anything else. No time for exploring myself and what else I could do in my life. Don't get me wrong, it wasn't an awful existence. I earned good money, experienced many different adventures and enjoyed some really rewarding times. However, I felt like a pre-programmed machine, never breaking out of myself or seeing just what I could do in life. The right path beckoned me but scared me at the same time, so I didn't consciously think about it, until that realisation, that day in my office.

Sound familiar? Do you ever wonder what you are capable of?

What the right path could hold? I hope so. If you don't, then now's the time to start.

So ... which path do you choose? It *is* your choice after all. I want you to make a decision now ... do you wish to travel down the right road?

Make the decision to take the right path. I dare you! If you feel uncertain, terrified, confused ... if you have an uncomfortable reaction, or feel anxious in just imagining doing something different ... or if really striding out along the right path scares you, then join the elite club of being alive ... really alive.

Go back now to the fork in the path and imagine yourself walking down the right path ... you walk into being a successful woman ... notice what you are wearing, your posture, your sparkling eyes, the confidence in your expression ... and then ... what else do you notice that makes this path the right one for you?

Embellish, exaggerate even, the you that walks along the right path, and in immersing yourself into this, become aware of greater inner peace, inner confidence, inner balance ... and also notice what else tells you that you are on the right path.

How was that?

You do know that just in immersing yourself like this, you will be altering your body's internal state, don't you? This has to happen as it's how your brain operates. As you imagine immersing yourself on your new path, your chemical profile and your neurological processes will alter, because you are doing, creating and sensing something different. A link will be forged between the new images you are generating and your biology and, in time, these will be cemented within you, bringing different actions and outcomes as if they had always been so. You are beginning the permanent altering of your inner biological atmosphere. *This* is genuine change at your inner core level!

You don't need will-power, because this change is happening with your whole neurology and psychology, and this will powerfully resonate in your sense of self, so it's not your thinking that you consciously have to change - *You* change at a fundamental level! Trying to simply use will-power means you are still consciously focusing on the unhelpful ways of thinking, *trying* to think something differently. It's coming from the wrong place. It's rather like the malaise of dieting: in focusing on what you need to be eating to lose weight, you are also focusing on what you are *not* eating, and what you *can't* eat, but want to! This creates a biological and psychological state of denial which is painful and unpleasant and could be said "counter-intuitive," and ultimately your will-power won't be able to override it, or will do, but only temporarily, at best.

This visualisation is not only creating the motivation for an inner state change, it's asking you to open up within you and become aware of the feeling of your life as it is now, and the feeling of your life as it can be: the feelings that pervade your very essence, your everyday experience no matter where you are or what you are doing. Once you have *all* the facts, you can then make an informed decision and evoke the power of your deep inner self.

Your present background is the feelings that you got when you imagined nothing changing when travelling down the "left path" for the next ten years. These may be a sense of distance, detachment, isolation, indifference, aloneness, disconnectedness, emptiness, and discontentment.

You may not have noticed this before, as most of the time we are externally focused, preoccupied by what's going on in our lives. But from now on, you have the ability to be aware of the backdrop against which all of your life is happening. So take a look and see what atmosphere is swirling around within you and imagine how different it will be, if you take the right path.

In imagining the right path, what new background did you experience? Engagement? Freedom? Aliveness? ... Or something else?

- Write a paragraph that summarises this for you ...

You are opening yourself up into an exciting journey, one that you are experiencing one step at a time. Imagine and explore the right path every day ... it *will* make the difference in your new beginning.

If not now ... when?

Our Methods

So, to the technicalities of how this change will occur.

My Success Programme is a unique integration of Neuro-Linguistic Programming (NLP), guided imagery and existential thinking.

NLP is one of the most powerful models of change ever invented which aimed, and succeeded, at discovering how to model incredibly successful people in order to show that if one person could do something amazing, then another could follow their strategies for success, to achieve the same. It teaches people how to learn, communicate and motivate themselves and others, and how to change behaviour. The goal in all of this is about striving for excellence. It states a connection between neurological processes (neuro), language (linguistic) and behavioural patterns, that have been learned through experience (programming). NLP has been around since the 1970's and has been integrated into more and more areas of everyday life over the last few years.

Amongst the many facets of human behaviour it "unpacks," NLP offers a number of principles to live and work by. They are called *pre-suppositions*, as they presuppose something to be true in the way human beings operate, which have been gleaned through the study of behavioural excellence. They are a set of assumptions that can guide you to successful and positive outcomes in your life should you wish to adopt them. Throughout this book I will be introducing you to a handful of them, giving you the opportunity to hugely maximize your potential.

You have already been subtly introduced to one of the NLP presuppositions, this being, "There's no failure, only feedback." In the fork in the road visualization, I encouraged you to be curious and inferred that there was no right or wrong way to do it. Hold this presupposition from now on in your life, and use all your experiences as a chance for feedback to learn something new. Remember clearly, *there is no failure, only feedback.*

A mental image can be defined as something that we create in the mind that we can mentally see, taste, smell, touch or feel; a thought with sensory qualities, if you like. The term *guided imagery* refers to a wide range of techniques including a simple visualisation of you doing something differently, or a metaphor or symbolic image that you are guided into, that represents an aspect of you, like imagining how you feel as the weather or as an animal. Here, elements of your unconscious are invited to appear as images that can communicate with the conscious mind. Imagery has the built-in capacity to deliver multiple layers of complex, encoded messages from your unconscious mind, by way of simple symbolic representation, to your conscious mind, aiding self-awareness: brain, mind, and body, connecting quite brilliantly.

Existential thinking is where you engage in considering your existence in the world, thinking about your life and perhaps life in general. This book will give you the opportunity to think about life, your meaning and purpose in it, what it is like to be you in the world, and the implications of your behaviour and choices. *This* will be engaging you in existential thinking.

Bonus Number 2

As much of this book is based on NLP, here for you now is my special Bonus Number 2. So that you can start learning about NLP, and how it can help you make powerful changes (alongside this book), I am giving you my *free* eBook on NLP. To get your copy, simply go to www.SandraWestlandMedia.com, download it and enjoy learning even more.

> Knowing your true self will help you work
> more effectively to reach your goals.
> It will lead you down the road to success.
> **~ Ritu Ghatourey ~**

How to Use This Book

You may have read a lot of books about self-development inviting you to dip in and out of each chapter and find what works for you. This isn't one of them. In writing this book, I take you through a process, with each chapter building on the last chapter, starting with the present moment in time and then taking you into your future. So turn each page as they come, and enjoy the journey.

I will accompany you through exploring your place in life as a woman, and into your inner minds' processing. From gaining greater knowledge about yourself, I will take you through a process of alignment; into forming an outcome as to how you want life to be that fits with your passion, so that you can achieve it, and thoroughly enjoy the journey along the way. I want you to enjoy the journey, as the journey is your life. You will learn along the way a variety of techniques to help change old habits, and unhelpful reactions to situations and people, so that the journey to Ultimate Success is organised from the inside out and the outside in.

Remember learning to drive a car? First, everything was clunky, awkward and mistimed even, where you had to consciously say to yourself the order of operation, something like *mirror, signal, brake, manoeuvre,* but gradually after a few stallings, failed hill starts, some kangarooing down the road (I am talking from experience), your actions and responses became less conscious and more natural, until eventually driving simply became a "part" of you, stored in your unconscious mind as a programme to run, every time you got in a car and drove. This is what will happen for you in following my Success Programme. It will become second nature and it will become natural.

Each chapter has "workouts." These are things to think about, things to imagine, things to observe yourself doing, and things to practice and refine. My advice is to give everything a go, and keep being curious. All of the exercises in this book I use myself, to keep learning and growing. They work.

Take your time, as it's a fascinating journey into the differing layers and depths that you have. Open up to yourself as you take part and complete your workouts. Write as much of it down as you can. You can either go to my website (www.SandraWestlandMedia.com) and download the workbook, or you can get yourself a journal to record your thoughts, and then your thoughts *about* those thoughts, and then how you feel about those! I want you to get in touch with all you are, and writing helps you really get to a deeper place within you. In writing down your thoughts and feelings during your journey through this book, you will have a much richer experience, and get from the book the most that you can.

At the end of each chapter, I'll ask you to record three things that you are going to focus on, or do. Please write something down at that stage, and keep referring back to it. Read the things that you write down a couple of times a week and see what a difference it makes.

As with any self-exploration, realisations may surface that perhaps you were not expecting. If they do, this is an opportunity to look at them and work with them. This may not be possible initially on your own, so I strongly advise you seek some additional help. Hypnotherapy, NLP, psychotherapy and counselling are all effective ways of working through things. If you can find someone that combines all of these approaches, then you will do yourself a big favour. Please remember that this book is not meant to be a substitute for therapy or coaching, but is designed to ignite a spark of excitement from within you, and move you towards your potential.

Who in the world am I?
Ah, that's the great puzzle.
~ Lewis Carroll, Alice in Wonderland ~

Chapter 2
Let's Think Outside of The Box
What am I not aware of, that I know?

At the centre of your being you have the answer;
you know who you are and you know what you want.
~ Lao Tzu ~

What is The Glass Ceiling?

Imagine a glass ceiling hovering above you, with *up* being your way ahead. The ceiling or barrier is see-through, so you can clearly observe those above who are more powerful, and see your own success there, but instead of being able to reach success, you are stopped by an invisible force that prevents you from rising further and reaching higher.

Let's go back now to the fork in the road visualisation again. Imagine a glass wall, between you and the road ahead. You can see where you want to go on the right road, you may even be able to see yourself in your successful future, but you simply can't get there, as the glass, the barrier, is preventing you. *This* is your glass ceiling!

The term "glass ceiling" has traditionally represented the unofficial barrier women have faced in the workplace, when looking to rise up the ladder to senior and executive positions. This glass ceiling has been seen as preventing women through stereotypical attitudes and institutional, or cultural, biases. You may have even experienced this yourself. I wonder just how you managed this and what impact it had on you?

In my twenty-five years of education and performance training, and my one-to-one work with women in senior management positions, I see something much more significant than this glass ceiling however; I see someone's very own *inner* glass ceiling holding them back.

Rebecca Shambaugh (2008), who wrote *It's Not a Glass Ceiling, It's a Sticky Floor*, also notes a similar experience:

> Decades of research continue to prop up the glass ceiling theory. And I don't disagree that there are still cultural impediments in business and society. But as I've worked with women and organizations for the last two decades to cultivate women leaders, I often see something else that is also part of this dilemma. I see women holding themselves back far more than society ever could. And they usually do it to themselves quite unknowingly. (pg. x)

This glass ceiling is based upon personal life history, and the subtle influences of societal views, as well as cultural ideologies that have been absorbed and personalised, and which together create self-limiting ways of being.

It may well be that your inner glass ceiling is mainly there for your protection; protection from the challenges and difficulties that unconsciously you perceive are a product of success. But with the Ultimate Programme, you will no longer need such protection, as these challenges will become expected and enjoyable realities, and ones that will nourish your living of life and propel you forward.

We could debate at length, and in different contexts, about *the* traditional glass ceiling but this will not likely change how you are in the world. The very fact that many women have chosen not to be held back by this, means that it is possible for *any* woman not to, should they choose! Think Anita Roddick, Karren Brady, Marissa Mayer, Oprah Winfrey, J.K Rowling, Stella McCartney and Vivienne Westwood for example. *They* have not been defined by *the* glass ceiling.

However, what *is* important to consider is how you have unconsciously "engraved" stereotypical gender biases (from the traditional glass ceiling) into the shards that make *your* ceiling. In exploring what you have absorbed unconsciously and how this influences your thoughts, feelings and behaviours, you will have greater awareness as to the natural you and thus greater choice as to how you are as a successful woman. Let's think about this, and delve further through the following exercise.

Exercise 2: Finding Unintentional Prejudgments About Women and Men

Explore the following and then complete the table at the end.

If I ask you now to think about a successful woman ... what image comes into your mind? What sort of person would that be?

Similarly, if I ask you now to think about a successful man ... what image comes into your mind? What sort of person would that be?

You may be hard pushed not to have stereotyped or learned prejudicial information in some way or another about these roles. You would have learned these ideas at an early age, before you were able to think about the information critically. So let's explore what your prejudicial thinking is, and reflect on how it informs and supports your current glass ceiling, and influences your behaviours.

Now complete the following table:

A Successful Women	How they look.	
	Their character or personality that I assume they have.	
	The behaviour that I would expect of them. Where have these ideas come from?	
A Successful Man	How they look.	
	Their character or personality that I assume they have.	
	The behaviour that I would expect of them. Where have these ideas come from?	

How do these ideas influence/impact how I am in the world? E.g., Do you believe that businesswomen should be tough and hard, and thus you are behaving in this way?

What would you like to do differently? How are you going to make a start at doing this?

For you as a unique individual, there is *history* and there is your *personal* history. You are the product of countless generations of lived years and lived eras, the creation of differing political, sociological and scientific views and the outcome of your younger formative years and family philosophies. You are complex! There are layers and layers of you, which may lead you to being confused as to how you really feel, or you might notice contradictions, or are struggling to explain your intentions and motivations. If so, then don't be surprised. We have some unravelling to do!

In my early work life, at a conscious level, if you had asked me, I would have said that I thought women and men were pretty much equal in the workplace. However, at a deeper level, just within the scope of my awareness, I would have been able to catch sight of myself feeling that women were in fact stronger, and more powerful than men. I certainly *felt* more in control of myself: more focused and driven in what I wanted to do, than most men I had come across. So, in my early career, I thought I was just doing my thing, working as hard as I could, going for promotions whenever they arose, with an inner competitiveness, and toughness.

However, on another level which was out of my awareness, I also wanted to be identified with men more than women, because my prejudicial thoughts were that women were the weaker sex, and I didn't want to be considered weak! So at one level I felt a woman; more powerful than a man, yet at another level, women were weak! I had taken in, from my formative years, that women were emotional (thus weak) and vulnerable, and I certainly didn't want to be considered in that way. So, as a Physical Education teacher I engaged whole heartedly in teaching rugby, cricket, football, as well as dance, netball and gymnastics, and I got out and put away heavy trampolines, and large pieces of gym equipment, without much thought. I tried to be what I considered "manlike," one of "the boys," to prove I was competent and strong, and thus "capable." I was acting from my more unconscious prejudicial beliefs. Yet also I held that women were in fact more powerful!

Confused? ... *So was I!*

I certainly was not being my real self, although I was not aware of this. All I had was a nagging feeling of being a fraud. I was dis-identifying with being a *traditional* woman (in my thinking) and yet secretly desiring to *be* a woman, as I *felt* the more powerful gender.

What are you thinking *now* about your own stereotypical gender based biases?

We are at the end of this chapter now, and are considering how unconsciously you might have pre-judged women and men, and the impact this has on you.

Consider:
> What has surprised you?
> What will you focus on, or ponder about regarding yourself over the next few weeks?
> What will you explore or try out?

I am going to ask you to write down three things now, so that you take ownership of your reflections, and move them into action. Remember, just in thinking about it, you are imagining it; in writing it down, you *embody* it and *there* begins the inner change process.

What I'm going to focus on is:

1)
2)
3)

The biggest problem that women have is being ambivalent about their own power. We should be comfortable with the idea of wielding power. We shouldn't feel that it detracts from our femininity.
~ Ingrid Bergman ~

Chapter 3
You Are The Force
May the force be with you

It does not matter how you came into the world,
what matters is that you are here.
~ Oprah Winfrey ~

Being Responsible

We exist. I guess nobody can argue with that!

We didn't ask to be born and we didn't request to whom, where or what situation we were born into. We had no say in what genes we inherited, and what we didn't. These are all *givens* as we enter the world, the facts of your life of which you can't change. The rest - how you choose to live your life as an adult - is up to you. This is not all that straightforward, as our childhood learnings are unconsciously embedded, defining to a large extent how we are, how we think, perceive, make meaning, behave and act in the world.

> The real voyage of discovery consists not in
> seeking new landscapes but in having new eyes.
> **~ Marcel Proust ~**

In my early working life, I had a strong perfectionist side that I would have said, at the time, was me simply wanting to do a high quality job. However, this side of me used to be full of anxiety, driving me to work incredibly hard, paying *maximum* attention to detail in my striving to make things perfect. It was relentless and exhausting. Eventually I was willing to take responsibility and recognise I was over doing things, and then I stopped and reflected. This led me to finding out where this driving force was coming from, and why it was so crucial to get everything right.

When I was nine years old, due to a serious car accident, my mum was recovering from brain damage, which meant that it was crucial to keep her calm. The only way to do this, I thought at the time, was to make sure everything was perfect. That way, life was predictable and she would remain calm. Also at that time, I was competing in piano competitions, where every piece played *had* to be performed perfectly. You can see where my perfectionist side came from, and why it was so full of anxiety - the anxiety about keeping my mum calm, and the anxiety of performing in front of so many people. I didn't need that same perfection in my thirties! So upon exploring and realising this, my perfectionism naturally toned down, as the anxiety from the past receded. I still strive (not drive) to do high quality work and I don't often make mistakes, but when I do, it's not catastrophic or life threatening. Actually, for me now, life is more about getting something done well, not perfect, and being able to move on in the scale of what I want to achieve, which is so much more important.

A previous client of mine, exploring how she was such a perfectionist in the workplace, told me about her boss remarking, "You give me a Rolls Royce, when in fact I only want a Mini." - No disrespect to Minis, of course, my first car was a Mini! - she didn't understand what her boss was meaning or what she was asking her to do as, "Why have a Mini when you could have a Rolls Royce?" she said.

The main deal of being human is that we are responsible for what we do in life, and what we don't do, and we are responsible for how we are and how we react to any situation. I was responsible for the perfectionist side that was driving me to exhaustion, for going for promotions or not, for changing career paths. I am responsible for writing this book and I am responsible for what I have decided to put in it for example. In fact, it is so much easier if we are willing to take ownership of our own lives, because that way we can do something about it, *we* can open ourselves up to doing something different if it's not working out for us.

This dawning happened for me when I was struggling to complete my master's dissertation on self-deception, funnily enough! On numerous occasions I became frustrated and annoyed about all the reasons why this was so difficult to complete. This particular day ... it was the university's fault, the amount of other work I had to do as well as write my dissertation, the day to day running of my house, the ironing ... you name it, I was coming up with any excuse possible. And in those moments it dawned on me. I recognised that whatever excuses I made and whoever I blamed, it was still completely down to me if I finished it or not. It made no difference to the university, or anyone else if I did or did not complete; it only made a difference to me. I was responsible for gaining my master's degree or not. It was *my* choice and my choice alone. Once I acknowledged this and took ownership of my own master's degree, I began to write it.

How does the prospect of taking complete ownership and responsibility of your life feel?

> In the long run, we shape our lives,
> and we shape ourselves.
> The process never end's until we die.
> And the choices we make are ultimately our own
> responsibility.
> ~ *Eleanor Roosevelt* ~

Your Philosophies of Life

I wonder what philosophies you hold about life and what happens in it. By that, I mean, do you believe in destiny or fate? "It was going to happen," or, "It's my destiny to fail," or do you believe that life is predetermined, planned out or that there is such a thing as karma: "What goes around comes around," or that we are fixed in our personality? "I start things and don't finish them … that's just me." Or do you believe that you will never rid yourself of a past trauma and that this is your lot in life, "It's because I was bullied at school"?

Whatever you fundamentally believe about what it is to be human, and what it is to be you, will certainly impact and influence what you do in life, including how much freedom you give yourself, and what excuses you allow yourself, for not making it, or fulfilling your dreams.

There are things in life you have no control over, but the *meaning* you give to your life - how you make it your own, and how you are able to meet the challenges that will occur along the way - you *are* able to choose and these *are* your responsibility. We are constrained by circumstances in many situations, but we are free to choose how we respond to those. We are free to *choose* to be more patient, more empathic, or less angry for example.

Two women, whom I met on one of my training courses, had both just found out that they had been made redundant from their jobs. One expressed feelings of depression, worrying about paying the mortgage and the bills, and wondering how she would ever find future employment, while the other woman described this very same event as an opportunity to do something different with her life, to re-train, or to take some time out to travel. They both showed the notion of being response-able in different ways, but they chose different responses and applied different meaning to the event. We are free to blame others for what happens to us, or can blame ourselves, or simply take responsibility for our situation and *do* something with it.

You can use a challenge to awaken you, or you can allow it to pull you into even deeper sleep.
~ Eckhart Tolle ~

Thus our assumptions about life, and meaning, underlie our very actions, and create and steer us through our lives. Considering the human condition and opening the door to philosophical debates with yourself is essential, crucial in fact, for you to gain a greater sense of you and what makes you tick.

Exercise 3: Your Philosophies of Life

When you have had something unexpected and challenging happen in your life:

a) How did you react and what did you do?
b) How did you explain why it happened?

From the above, consider:

- What are your philosophies of life? (Destiny? Luck? Something else?)
- How have you come to this conclusion?
- How does this determine how you live your life?
- Is it a helpful philosophy?
- How open are you to there being other possibilities?
- How responsible do you feel for you; how much ownership do you take of your life?

Existential Anxiety – The Freedom

Have you ever caught yourself imagining just what you could do in life, given the right time, circumstances, and finances?

When I went within myself and thought about it, and allowed my thoughts to travel into such wondering, initially I had a big fat nothing! But then, in revisiting this after *that* morning in my office, before teaching Badminton, I found I was quickly becoming anxious. Giving myself permission to do anything I wanted, meant there were actually *no* limits, and that took my breath away. There were indeed endless possibilities, and I felt overwhelmed by knowing such freedom. We call this "existential anxiety," a worry, dread or panic that arises from the contemplation of life's biggest questions such as "Who am I?" or "Why am I here?" or "What is my meaning in life?" This is very different to our *everyday* anxiety, such as being anxious about public speaking, because you might freeze, or anxious about missing the train, or being late for work.

Let's see this in action: *The scenario is* - I am thinking of handing my notice in at work and starting up my own business.

Everyday anxiety, will lead me to saying, "Oh my goodness, why am I thinking of starting up my own business? I can't, I'm not good enough … what will people think? …. What if it doesn't work? … How will I manage? … What happens if I make a mistake? Why am

I thinking it might work? I'm anxious and scared of failing. I had better not hand my notice in."

Existential anxiety, will sound more like, "Oh my goodness ... I'm thinking of handing my notice in ... I could start my own business ... I've not done that before, anything could happen ... There will be a lot to learn, but I'm going to see what happens ... What have I got to lose? It's going to be an adventure. I'm going to do this! I'm anxious, and nervous, as I don't know just what will happen and I am responsible for that, which actually makes me feel panicky ... but excited about how things will evolve. Let's get that resignation letter written!"

Existential anxiety is an inevitable part of being alive, and is the result of knowing that we are free and responsible in the creation of our own lives, and for the uncertainty this brings. If we can embrace living within it, and alongside it, we can experience a greater authentic way of being. Existential anxiety won't cripple you, but will move you to a richer living of life, and open you up to your possibilities, and potential. Imagine being able to dream about doing anything you want and then making it happen.

Everyday anxiety *will* prevent you from doing all manner of things; it will stop you in your tracks, and cause you to avoid situations, people, and promotions. It allows you to hide from the existential anxiety, the right kind of anxiety that you need to learn to be with, as herein lays your passions, your potential and your personal road to growth.

Exercise 4: Existential Anxiety

Daydream for a moment. Imagine just what you could do in life, given the right time, circumstances and finances.

What happens?

- Can you identify and pinpoint existential anxiety?
- What things come to mind that you want to do? Write a novel? Start your own business? Travel? Something else?
- Make a list and refer to it regularly.

In beginning to embrace the responsibility we have for ourselves, the freedom and choices we have and can make, we now need to turn to exploring something fundamental and influential in all of this ... This being our existence in this world as a woman.

Being a Woman

This won't come as a big shock, but being a woman is different to being a man! Genetically, this difference is around one percent, which doesn't sound a lot, but just think about being on a cruise liner heading across the Pacific Ocean! If you drift one percent off course, you will end up in a very different place than you intended. One percent is a lot!

This one percent genetic difference will influence every cell in your body, which means the way you experience pleasure, pain, perception, thinking, feeling and emotions, to name but a few, will be different. Women have different brain sensitivities to stress and conflict; hence we will experience them differently. We have ten percent more neurons for language and hearing than men, and the hippocampus (the part of the limbic system that plays an important role in long-term memory) is also larger in women's brains. There are many fascinating differences hardwired into us that differentiate our gender. For further information, read *The Female Brain* by Louann Brizendine (2007) - it's a really interesting read.

Brizendine states that the female brain has:

Tremendous unique aptitude, outstanding verbal agility, the ability to connect deeply in friendships, a capacity to read faces and tones of voice for emotional states of mind and the ability to diffuse conflict. These are hardwired into the brains of women. These are the talents women are born with. (pg. 31)

Do you recognise yourself in this description?

Our hardwiring is one thing, and even this will be different for each one of us, but add within your own personal history, and we have a totally unique and individual woman, a woman, moreover, with bags of natural talent.

What needs to be considered now then is how *you* experience being a woman.

I think for me, one of the most profound turning points in my personal development was embracing and exploring being a woman, in my own unique way. In my twenties, I didn't think about what it was like being me through my sexuality. As a Physical Education teacher, I wore a tracksuit most of the time, no make-up or much of a hairstyle, and rarely was I seen in a skirt or anything that could remotely be stereotyped as feminine. My journey into embodying, experiencing, expressing and enjoying being a woman has been a curious, profound, enjoyable and an ever continuing journey - a journey of personal empowerment.

Exercise 5: How are You, with Being a Woman?

Notice the messages that come from your body as you explore the following:

- How do you express yourself as a woman? By that I mean, what clothes do you wear? What about accessories? What makes you choose how you present yourself to the world?

- Do you feel comfortable with that?

- How do you feel and react around other women?

- How do you feel and react around men?

- How do you feel about your female body, and how it looks, and how it works?

- Would you like to change anything from the above that would allow you to really be you?

This is quite some deep exploration, so take your time. There is a need to accept what you can't change, embrace what you can, and enjoy being the woman you are.

Please drop me a line now on my feedback page www.SmashingYourGlassCeilingFeedback.com and let me know how it is for you, being a woman, at this time. I really want to know. *Together* let's build the story of what it is to be a woman. There you will also find out how other women are with this, through my social media links.

Modelling Successful Women

Pre-supposition 1: If one person can do something, other people can learn from that person's success.

The idea of modelling is well known in NLP. It looks to explore the thoughts, behaviours, skills, beliefs, values and other qualities, that exceptionally successful people have. The principle is that in learning about the success behaviours of someone else, we can incorporate some of their methods into our own behavioural repertoire, so as to enable us to achieve our own goals too. We can model exactly what they *do*, not to become *them*, but to accelerate us into our own way of successful being, so we can enhance our own achievements in whatever it is that we are striving for.

We are looking to gain as much information as we can about how to be a successful woman, so, the questions to explore are:

- Which women in business do you admire, or would like to model?
- Which women inspire you, in general?

Let's have a look at some examples.

Karren Brady was born in 1969. She became the managing director of Birmingham City Football Club at just twenty-three years of age, and is currently vice-chairman of West Ham United. She was responsible for the company's flotation in 1997, thus becoming at the time, the youngest managing director of a UK Plc. She describes herself as hard working, a straight talker, and someone who doesn't let people put her down. She does things with purpose, knowing what she wants out of a situation, playing to her strengths and using her skills in the best possible way. For her, success is about understanding who you are, and what you want out of life. She is a woman who stands up for women's rights, and believes that the best companies in the world contain a mixed and diverse combination of people. She uses her profile to effect change and raise awareness, helping to address issues that infringe on women's rights to equality.

(Dame) Valerie Beral was born in 1946. She is described as a breast cancer pioneer. I am wondering if you have ever heard of her. She is one of the pioneers of the Million Women Study, the largest study in the world, which was started in 1997, with one in four women in the UK in the target age group participating. The study has recruited more than 1.5 million UK women over fifty years of age. Valerie is passionate about the health of women, and never forgets this when she and her research is challenged and criticized. The study she co-founded investigates how women's reproductive history affects their health, focusing on the consequences of taking hormone replacement therapy (HRT). Her evidence has played a dramatic part in the move for HRT to be halved and thus 10,000 women who may have developed breast cancer, to be saved from this ordeal. Even though she has been challenged constantly on her research, and attacked from many quarters, she looks to the bigger picture, the reason she is doing this. She is doing it for women, and women's health!

There are many more inspirational women and inspirational businesswomen, but I want you to delve into this yourself and find those women that move something in you … Think about the women making a difference in the world, and find who you are drawn too.

Exercise 6: Modelling Successful Women

Take three women that inspire you and answer the following questions for each one.

What exactly do they do that inspires you?	
How do they do it?	
When do they do it?	
Where do they do it?	

Who do they do it with?	

Now summarise what you have written above, combining all of the qualities and behaviours you've recorded into one summarising paragraph.

Once you have noted just what it is that you want to model, spend some time exploring how you would do this in your own way. It needs to be congruent.

The women you are drawn to, and that inspire you, will hold the qualities that you actually have, even if you don't recognise them yet as your own. In *NLP at Work,* Sue Knight (2008) writes, "If you spot it, you've got it". In being able to recognise a quality in another person, it means you can represent it in your own mind, therefore you are capable of it too. So tap into yourself and find those qualities through modelling how these women are. Adopt these qualities *as if* they are your own. Aspire to be what you yourself admire. Now is your chance, *take it!*

Now you have recognised the qualities from modelling excellence. Let's put this into your own personal scenario.

Passion is energy. Feel the power that
comes from focusing on what excites you.
~ Oprah Winfrey ~

Exercise 7: The Amazing Miracle Scenario!

The next thing to become familiar with is *exactly* how it will be, when you are successful. No maybe, possibly, or perhaps, but a real sense of what, how, with who and when you will have the ultimate success, and how that will be. My clients and groups are often left bemused by this question at first, as they think they already have this one covered! They think they know the successful them, yet have never truly envisaged, vividly, what that would actually be like.

So, imagine that after reading this chapter, you sense something amazing happening within you. You then go to sleep, and in the morning awaken to notice that during the night, something incredible has occurred. Overnight you have become a successful woman!

Let's answer a few questions:

1) What is the first thing you notice that tells you are successful? You wake up, and bang! What is the first thing that *really* springs out to you?

2) What are you able to do now, that you couldn't do before, that tells you definitively that you *are* successful?

As we move on to this question, we begin to look at how this change affects the wider areas of your life. What are you able to do that you couldn't do before … and in what different situations does this change affect you, and what is it like?

3) Imagine as you go through the rest of your day. What happens as you get out of bed, have breakfast, go to work, take lunch, finish work, go home, enjoy your evening and then retire to bed?

This step begins to make your awareness real. It brings the change into actual everyday situations. This formulates and operates the running of a new internal movie. We begin to see what was normal before, like how you got out of bed, prepared and had breakfast, began your working day, and managed that day, through the differences that now have happened.

4) Begin to be aware of not only your reaction to these situations, but also to who else notices that you are successful. Imagine people seeing you in this way. What tells *them* that this amazing change has happened?

Now we move out of your own experience and into others' experience of you, as a successful woman. This can be a powerful insight. When you ask the questions, "How have I looked to others?" and then, "How do I look now as a successful woman?", then you are a step closer to actually *living* that success. So, ask yourself, *who* notices you? What do they see you doing? How might it be for them to see you like this? Asking these questions really takes you out of yourself, and gets you to think of *you* as a person, experienced by others.

Put into words just *how* things will be. Write it down as if you are already there. This will help your mind begin to search for moments when you have what you want, and also to create opportunities where you will have it, for real. It expands your conscious and unconscious expectations beyond the specifics and out into the bigger picture. It widens the context in which the miracle has happened. That way, it is more in line with you as a whole person. Don't say "I imagine that …," say things here such as "I feel …," and "I am …"

Your Inner Glass Ceiling

Pre-supposition 2: Behind every behaviour there is positive intention.

I would like you to become really curious, as you begin to explore further your inner glass ceiling with me. If for any reason you have an inclination to be judgemental or harsh on yourself, just postpone

43

that for a while, because if you can understand just what your ceiling is all about, then you can and will transform it into a platform, a springboard, even.

At the moment you are holding an image of you in the future *with* your inner glass ceiling in place. All present actions and decisions are made with its influence. For example, if within it is the belief that you don't think you can achieve much, or you don't deserve success, then you will work and base decisions from this position. What we need to do is to begin to discover your *true* self-image, one where there is no ceiling, or anything holding you back.

Exercise 8: Finding What's in Your Glass Ceiling

We are going to explore through a visualisation again. So get relaxed and clear your mind. Make sure you have the time and space to develop the images, and explore them.

1) Imagine standing on a line that represents time for you, or even better, actually find a bit of space around you now, and physically stand on an imagined line in the room. Stand in the present so that the past is behind you and the future ahead of you. Reach out and point to each aspect of time if it helps. Get a real *felt* sense of this.

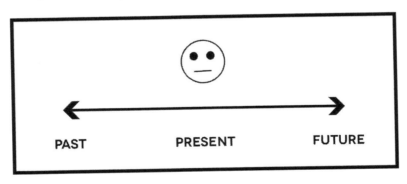

Now, answer these questions:

- How does the future seem to you?
- How does the past seem to you?
- Is there anything that you notice, or that surprises you about the past and future, on this line of time?

2) Now look into the future and see the *you* of the future, who has achieved success, and has all the resources you could possibly need, to live a full and happy life. Here you can meet challenges, face setbacks, and have fun. Here you are wise, centred … and you have everything you want. You are *all* you really want to be. You have opened up to all the inner resources that you naturally have and need.

As you stand in the present with the future you ahead, get a real felt sense of the threshold you must cross, the glass ceiling that you must smash through to get there.

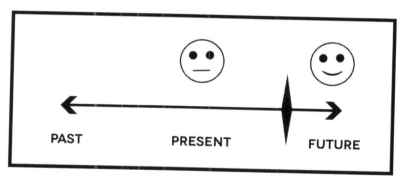

Now, answer these questions:

- What words would you use to describe that barrier, your glass ceiling?
- What is holding you back?
- What is the *positive intention* of this barrier? Why or how might it be helping you in some way?

Let me explain what positive intention means. In NLP terms, every behaviour has a positive intention behind it. So, if you suffer from panic attacks, which originated from a fear of making a fool of yourself, in having panic attacks *now*, you won't go to that conference and potentially make a fool of yourself, or you won't go to that social gathering, so you won't make a fool of yourself there either. So the positive intention of panic attacks is to prevent you from making a fool of yourself. For somebody who "comfort eats" - the positive intention will be to make themselves feel better. The positive intention in reading this book may be to set yourself free from blocks that are holding you back. So what is the positive intention of your glass ceiling?

3) Now walk along your timeline and move into the future to the place where you get the felt sense of success and resourcefulness. "Try on" the future you. Step inside her and see what she's like. Then, look back at the present where you were struggling to smash the glass ceiling.

Answer these questions:

- Is there any further awareness about the glass ceiling now you have made it and are successful?
- What steps did you need to take to get to where you are?
- What would you say to yourself in the present that would be helpful?

4) Step out of the future you, and walk back along the time line, back to the present, bringing with you the knowledge and resources from the future position, and transfer them into the present you, of the now.

Take some time to reflect on this experience.

Now ... with this new information ... What is holding you back?

What is the positive intention of having the glass ceiling for you? To avoid failure, rejection, or abandonment? To not experience embarrassment? Is it too freeing and un-tethered? Do you not want to take the responsibility for yourself? Or something else?

You need to find the positive intention for keeping you at the place in life where you are, because there *is* one. Once you have found it, then you can begin to examine the logic supporting it, and its current relevance, in the light of what you are now unearthing within you.

Having done this exercise with many people, there are often surprising results, and the knowledge that has been uncovered has been simply life changing, in itself.

> *Fiona* found out that she was scared of actually being successful. She wasn't sure she could handle such responsibility, and the potential failure she thought that would inevitably hold.

> *Sarah* found the glass (in the glass ceiling) was mainly that of her "shining", which she "translated" into her being arrogant and tiresome for others, inevitably leading to ultimate rejection.

Me? Well I know now that it was a fear of success. My positive intention was to protect me from all that success meant for me, which I translated into being out of my depth, not knowing what to do, and ultimately, therefore, messing it up, and getting it wrong!

So what's holding you back?

It's time now to reflect and take your learning forward.

What I'm going to focus on is:

1)
2)
3)

Let's take stock for a moment. Over the last few chapters ...

a) You have created a desire to move forward in your life, not just because if you stay where you are, it will be pretty average, but because moving forward will give you energy, excitement and a sense of fulfilment.

b) You are also pondering on the impact of what being a woman means to you and how your upbringing and society have influenced this. You are spending time considering how you are, curious at the things you do, how you present yourself, and the meaning of these. You are also exploring other successful women and women in business, to further your insights into how *you* want to be.

c) You are aware that you are responsible for the choices you make, and that existential anxiety is fundamentally present in your life, so you can embrace it, and embrace being alive.

d) You are exploring your glass ceiling and are now more conscious of what's kept you where you are thus far in life, and what will make a difference to you, in your future.

e) Finally you are rehearsing, and learning, about how it will be, in your awesome amazing future.

That's quite some journey so far!

Where next? Well, in order to have better control of your mind and behaviour, it's vitally important to understand how your inner mind processes information and for better communication, to understand how others process information too. In gaining greater insights into this, you will be able to manage yourself more effectively in the present, which will open you up to more of the bigger picture, as you will have more "inner space." If you don't have to worry so much, about getting annoyed with a client, or fluffing a meeting or interview, you can spend more time embracing your dreams and goals in life. So let's get intimate!

> Dare to dream of your great success. Become intimate with those things which deeply motivate you and regularly work toward the realization of that mission.
> **~ Mary Anne Radmacher ~**

Chapter 4
We need a little more due diligence here!
How is your inner mental processing?

If you talk to people in a language they
understand, that goes to their head.
If you talk to them in *their* language,
that goes to their heart.
~ Adapted from Nelson Mandela ~

If you want to be successful in your life, and in business, enjoying deeply enriching relationships, then embracing the fact that we are all uniquely different in our inner mental processing, and yet in many ways similar, is a must. Let's explore what I mean by this.

Presupposition 3: You cannot not communicate.

Communication and Rapport

It makes sense to me, that to be successful, you need to be able to communicate clearly, and have skilful versatility in your interactions with others, to build the quality relationships necessary for that success to grow. Communication is the very essence of how we connect with people. Rapport is the quality of that connection. Therefore, building rapport is crucial, if we are going to be successful. Without it, little of meaning happens.

When I go to my local train station to buy a ticket, I communicate with the person behind the ticket desk. Do I need to create rapport with them? Well, possibly! It depends if I want to get a good deal on my train fare. I could ask them if they are having a good day, enquire as to what they think might be the best deal of the day, in terms of my ticket price, or just smile, understandingly, at the previous awkward customer I have just heard them deal with, ahead of me in the queue. I don't have to do this. I could just turn up at the ticket desk, request my ticket and be on my way.

Rapport, though, enables me to get what I want (a good deal), and allows for a much more pleasant experience, for both me, and the person I'm communicating with. It forges a very brief, yet powerful connection, between me and the ticket seller, which changes, at a fundamental level, how the outcome of that communication will turn out. By communicating a vested interest in the ticket seller as a *person*, the outcome will be that they show an interest in *me* as a person, above that of somebody they are just selling a train ticket to. The ticket seller has someone interested in them as a person, treating them respectfully, and I get a good deal on my train ticket, and we *both* enjoy a few moments of genuine connection (rapport). Of course, if you lack genuine interest in others, and are only out for manipulating them for your own gain, then that's a different ball game altogether, because the *intention* is totally different. Actually, I believe rapport is impossible to falsely create. Have you ever experienced a salesperson cold calling you on the telephone, trying to sell you something, asking you in their opening statement, "Hi ... how are you today?" It doesn't quite work, does it? You can't help but sense the incongruence.

With quality rapport ...

- People naturally feel more connected with you.
- People feel comfortable around you.
- People understand your message more clearly.
- In sales you are more likely to convince the other to purchase *your* product or service.
- In leadership, you are more likely to be understood, and thus gain results.
- You gain better relationships all round!

This being the case, let's look at how you can create greater rapport with others.

People never forget how you made them feel.
~ *Maya Angelou* ~

My World is Different to Your World

Presupposition 4 – The map is not the territory.

Everybody sees the world differently. We all have our own structured "map" of the world, depending on our upbringing, our beliefs, prejudices, and individual perceptions, at any given time. We are more likely to achieve quality rapport, if we understand that the perception of the world that each of us has, is entirely different. The person you are communicating with may not be being awkward, naïve, or ignorant, if they don't seem to be understanding you: they simply have a different internal map to you.

Each one of us lives in our own unique reality, based on the inner filtering systems we have in operation. Just as you sit and read this paragraph, there is an extraordinary amount of data being absorbed through your senses, which you experience in your own personal way. This is why there is no *one* reality; there is only the reality based on how *you* filter what *you* experience, via your sensory channels.

You convert vast amounts of external data into internal images, sounds, feelings, tastes and smells, through your personally unique filters, which are then transformed into an internal map that reflects the outside world to you. This equals *your* reality.

For example, imagine you have "fear of making mistakes," as a filter. Imagine a filter as a pair of tinted glasses (rose coloured, if you like!), where you look out into the world with the view of "fear of making a mistake". The moment you see your boss entering the room, you view them through your filter, and a strong fear response is experienced instantly: the "what have I done wrong" reaction. Your neurological filter has at some point been trained to set off this response, before you have added any language to make sense of the situation, and consciously created meaning of the sensory experience. Your boss, after all, may simply be asking you out for lunch, or want to praise you for something you have done well.

When you *do* add language to your sensory experience, you are adding a certain quality and personal meaning to it, one that is also unique to you.

Think of a table ... To label an object as a table, you will have an internal visual representation in your mind of a table. In addition, you will have other internal representations for different categories of tables, such as a kitchen table, a dining room table, a work bench, office desk, bedside table, a table of contents, a times table, and so on. You will also have a kinaesthetic (feeling-based) internal representation for what it feels like to work on, or use these different types of table. You may have internal auditory (thought-talk), olfactory (smell) and gustatory (taste) representations as well, which may well take you to eating a meal from a dining room table.

If I then ask you to think of a "solid" table, you will then go on a further internal search, which NLP calls a "transderivational search," to re-present to yourself what you understand to be a solid table. We would likely all be able to categorise, or label, what a table is. However, what "looks solid" is a statement based on your own personal criteria for the idea of solid, which is based on past experience. Your criteria of solid may be completely different to mine. How many times have you heard of a "solid" relationship, turning out not to be so solid at all? So was it solid or not?

I hope you can see the subjectivity of our representations here, how they *are* just representations and how, for each one of us, it will be different.

So let's think about the word "appraisal". What reactions do you have? What does this word mean to you?

A boss may hold it as an opportunity to praise an employee's hard work, while the employee of that boss may experience it as a time when they expect to be criticized. Imagine how both will meet for the same appraisal meeting with very different expectations. We can never assume the meaning we assign to a situation will be the same as anyone else's.

The Representational Systems

The three main representational systems that we use to filter the experience of the world are those of the visual, auditory and kinaesthetic sensory modalities. The olfactory and gustatory sensory systems feature less in our experience, but are still naturally present, and we also use the auditory-digital representational system, which is our inner self-talk. While all three of the main systems are present in your map, at any given time, one is usually more dominant than the others. This is crucial to be aware of, as each representational modality comes with its own unique system of organising your experience of the world.

By learning how to distinctly detect the differing representational systems, and how they are operating in any given moment with another, you can quickly and effectively build and maintain rapport, and be more personally precise and influential in your communication. How? Well, once you are able to recognise others' representational systems, and the way *they* organise their maps, it means you can then adapt your language, and respond to them in a way that matches *their* sensory processes. When we match, it *feels* good. You will be amazed at how easily and quickly you can gain rapport with other people, through matching their personally preferred representational system. It's not a secret, but there are some very fundamental things you need to know, and do, to make skilful communication a natural and congruent part of your interpersonal interactions.

Let's look at this in more detail in terms of the different ways people communicate via their representational systems. Here are some examples:

A Visual Processing Person:

- Pays attention to their visual experience, predominantly working through internal images.
- Their language will be visually arranged, such as, "Do you *see* what I mean? Can you *picture* that? You have a *bright* future," and, "I *imagine* that this will be challenging."
- Tends to sit erect, looking upwards as they access their inner experiences, and breathes from their chest.
- Learns and memorizes by seeing pictures.
- Becomes bored in lectures without adequate visual stimulations.
- Can let go of emotions, as they organise their world visually.

- Often draws diagrams to "illustrate" their point of view.
- May make visual-based value judgements on how a person presents themselves, e.g. tidiness, clothes, hairstyle etc.
- Will be less aware of the other representational systems, and may even "delete" from awareness other systems, such as immediate sounds, or bodily sensations, or the feelings of others in relation to their "point of view".
- Uses gestures and pointing, to communicate, or emphasise key elements.
- Needs plenty of room in their field of vision, hence they can see things, so they need space when you are communicating with them!

So, to communicate effectively with a visual processing person, you would use visual language cues, you would sit up, use pictures to illustrate your point, and *look* the part!

An Auditory Processing Person:

- Hears their world predominantly through sounds and internal dialogue (auditory digital).
- Uses language that denotes sound, such as "tune in" and "sounds like".

- Memorizes steps, procedures and sequences, and will often talk to themselves.
- Breathes from the middle of the chest, and their speech is pronounced, and deliberate.
- Will tend to move their eyes sideways, and down to their left as they access their inner experiences.
- Values auditory feedback.
- Responds to tones of voice, likes to talk things through, and remembers verbal instructions.
- Makes judgments based on how things sound, and how the person they are listening to, sounds.
- Will concentrate on the minute sounds of an experience.
- Will learn by listening, and likes to be told the on-going process of things.
- Often makes hand gestures, or will point to their ears or rub their chins.
- May like to talk a lot and enunciate thoughts clearly, and with good sound quality.

In communicating with an auditory processing person, use auditory language, make sure you vary your tone of voice, and encourage them to talk. Deliver your message in bullet points, speaking clearly, and at a reasonable pace, and get them to think about things.

A Kinaesthetic Processing Person:

- Tends to look down and to the right as they access their inner experiences, and breathes low in the stomach. If they *feel* deeply, they will breathe deeply.
- Typically speaks slowly and uses long pauses.
- Experiences their world predominantly through their feelings and therefore they have high *body* awareness.
- Will use feelings-based language such as "get a grip," and, "I have a gut feeling."
- Is more connected with body sensations, touch, and the feeling of clothes on their body.
- Is more likely to use specific types of feelings to gauge decisions.
- Uses touch demonstratively, when communicating and emphasising key points.
- Enjoys movement, and hands on activities.
- Is motivated by physical rewards, like a pat on the back. They love closeness!
- Tends to find it difficult to break out of negative emotions.

So, in communicating with a kinaesthetically processing person, use feeling, and action words, speaking slowly, and encouraging them to feel and get a sense of things. Get them active, so pass things around for them to handle. Touch them on the shoulder, and shake their hand.

How are You in the World?

Think now about …

a) When you go into a meeting or social gathering … what is the first thing you notice?

- Is it how many people are present, or the room layout, or what people are wearing? If so, you are operating in a predominantly *visual* modality.

- If you immediately hear people's voices, or the music or any other noise, then you are predominantly an *auditory* organiser.
- If you sense the atmosphere, notice the temperature, the texture of chairs, or are aware of how your clothes feel, then you are working in the *kinaesthetic* modality.

b) When you are buying a piece of furniture, what do you do?

- Go into a shop and look at all the different designs, and imagine it in your home? (visual)
- Do you run your hand along the piece of furniture, and sense how it feels? (kinaesthetic)
- Do you have a conversation in your mind about what this piece of furniture is like, or sit on it, and hear how it sounds? (auditory)

Me? My world is very auditory. I won't buy a leather-type sofa, as I don't like the sound it makes as I sit down on it, or the noises it makes as I or others naturally move around on it. When buying furniture, I cannot visualise what it will look like, or if it will fit in the room intended. It has been known that I have bought furniture that doesn't actually fit in its intended room! An expensive lesson about representational systems, and the need to always take a *visual* friend when purchasing furniture!

Which of the senses is your primary system? Have you recognised it yet?

Let's make it even easier with the following Modalities Preference Test

Exercise 9: How are you in the world?

This is not a rigorously scientific test, but rather a generalised indicator, that will simply allow you to explore what representational systems you are mainly operating from.

For each of the following statements, place a number next to every phrase.

Use the following system to indicate your preference:

      4 = Closest to describing you.
      3 = Next best description.
      2 = Next best.
      1 = Least descriptive of you.

E.g. When on a beach holiday, the first thing that makes me smile is …

a. (2) The feel of the cool sand, the warm sun, or the fresh breeze on my face.
b. (4) The roar of the waves, the whistling wind, or the sound of birds in the distance.
c. (1) This is the type of holiday that makes sense, or the cost is reasonable.
d. (3) The scenery, the bright sun, and the blue water.

1) I make important decisions based on:

a. ( ) gut level feeling.
b. ( ) which way sounds best to me.
c. ( ) what looks best to me.
d. ( ) precise review, and study of the issues.

2) During an argument, I am most likely to be influenced by:

a. ( ) the other person's tone of voice.
b. ( ) whether or not I can see that other person's argument.
c. ( ) the logic of the other person's argument.

d. (   )   whether or not I feel I am in touch with the other person's true feelings.

3) I most easily communicate what is going on with me by:

a. (   )   the way I dress and look.
b. (   )   the feelings I share.
c. (   )   the words I choose.
d. (   )   the tone of my voice.

4) It is easiest for me to:

a. (   )   find the ideal volume when turning on a radio.
b. (   )   select the most intellectually relevant point, concerning an interesting subject.
c. (   )   select the most comfortable furniture.
d. (   )   select rich, attractive colour combinations.

5) Grade the phrases below:

a. (   )   I am very attuned to the sounds of my surroundings.
b. (   )   I am very adept at making sense of new facts and data.
c. (   )   I am very sensitive to the way articles of clothing feel on my body.
d. (   )   I have a strong response to colours, and to the way a room looks.

6) When I feel overwhelmed I find it helps to:

a. (   )   see the bigger picture.
b. (   )   talk or listen to another person.
c. (   )   get in touch with what is happening.
d. (   )   make sense of things, in my head.

7) One of my strengths, is my ability to:

We need a little more due diligence here!

a. ( )   see what needs to be done.
b. ( )   make sense of new facts and data.
c. ( )   hear what sounds right.
d. ( )   get in touch with my feelings.

Now copy your answers on to the table below.

	Visual	Auditory	Kinaesthetic	Auditory Digital (thought talk)
My Example:	D 3	B 4	A 2	C 1
1.	C	B	A	D
2.	B	A	D	C
3.	A	D	B	C
4.	D	A	C	B
5.	D	A	C	B
6.	A	B	C	D
7.	A	C	D	B
Totals : Don't include the example from the top.				
	Visual	Auditory	Kinaesthetic	Auditory Digital

The higher the score, the stronger the representational system is for you. Remember that if you scored high up on auditory-digital representation, it means that you are an analyser, you think and rationalise, and hold logic high in your way of processing information. Do you recognise this description?

Now think about the people you work with, or have worked with in the past. Include those people you get on well with, and those you just didn't seem to connect with, or get close to for some reason. This could be the time that you consider if they do, or do not have, the same main representation system as you. If you look at the descriptions above of the three different processing types, can you recognise the difference?

Imagine this scenario … An auditory team member leaves half-drunk cups of coffee on the table, their coat in the corner on the floor, and papers all over the place. A visual boss thinks that they are a total slob, who doesn't appreciate how important it is to have a "picture perfect" office, bemoaning, "If she respected me, she would understand and appreciate how important a tidy office is for an efficient and successful business."

On the flip side of this story, the auditory team member comes to her work space, her castle, her only desire being to get on with her work, and read her emails, in silence. But, oh no! All she hears is the sound of people on the phone, the boss chatting, the radio whining away in the background … It's impossible to focus on her task, and she complains, "Can't I get some peace and quiet at my own desk?"

Do you hear some misunderstandings taking place?

You'll probably recognize all three systems working within you across the different areas of your life, which is normal. You may also note that certain systems are more prominent in different areas of your life than others. You might, for example, be more visual at work (particularly if you are in a visually-orientated job, such as design), but perhaps you feel more attuned kinaesthetically at home, enjoying a good emotive film, curled up on your old soft comfy sofa, in your favourite "down-time" clothes.

If you note you are lacking in one system, it would be beneficial to enhance it, as increasing your flexibility in all the representational systems will make it easier to connect with more people. In enhancing your weaker system, you open up to more possibilities. More possibilities equal more choices. The key to communication is versatility. The more you know about the language that is being spoken in your communications, the more versatile you can be.

So, if you think you are not very visual, then you could take yourself to somewhere where you can really explore colours, shapes, and sizes, and accustom yourself to the world of abstract! When you read a book, imagine the scene in your mind; when you hear a piece of music, allow yourself to create an image of the sounds.

If you feel you are not auditory, then go into a garden and listen to the birds singing, picking out the different songs. Listen to different types of music and see what feelings it brings forth. Listen to the ticking of a clock and see what it brings to you. Or listen to one of the most amazing sounds available, the sound of silence. Where does *that* take you?

If you think you are not kinaesthetically attuned, then explore the textures of things. Touch your furniture, or the different surfaces around you. Touch your own skin or your facial features and sense how they feel. Hug a few friends (with their permission), or hug a tree (no permission needed, ordinarily), and see how it feels! Explore different temperatures, how clothes feel next to your skin, or touch an animal (preferably not a dangerous one!) and feel them move.

Presupposition 5:   *Genuine understanding only comes from experience - so act.*

The learning is in the doing, so test this all out.

During your next meeting, be it with your team at work, or with another colleague or friend, be aware of showing the visual processing people pictures and samples, to stimulate their visual senses. Allow the kinaesthetic processing people to hold or handle something, as they need to get a feel for what you are saying. The auditory processing people are motivated by sound, so be aware of the words you say, and if you can use something that creates an interesting sound, to get your point across, then let them hear the quality you have to offer, and make sure you let them pass comment. They *need* to! For an auditory digital processor, give them some data to analyse, and think about, and get them to consider the pros and cons of a situation.

Presupposition 6: The meaning of the communication is in the response you get.

So … take responsibility for *your* communications and for being understood. If the response you get is not what you are expecting, you can now change your mode of communication. You will be pleasantly surprised at the difference this makes.

Here is an extract from an email I received from a client of mine (permission to publish this has been given), who had attended one of my workshops on NLP. The email was entitled "Magic Happens!"

> *Following our NLP weekend, I decided to take daily opportunities at work to apply the skills I've learnt (to practice them) during my everyday one to one interactions. With active awareness, I observed people and tried to subtly mirror physical and verbal expressions to see if I could tune into their physical and internal states, and speak their language. I must admit, I was absolutely astonished by the results. Since starting this, I have been receiving quite regular feedback from my colleagues about how they feel surprisingly understood by me, which has contributed to making our professional rapport much stronger.*

However, what has really made it rather fascinating was the experience from yesterday with one of my senior engineering managers, who I would describe as very challenging to read, as he appears rather rigid in his body language. He approached me to discuss work related matters, however, as I consciously started to mirror him (which was very interesting in itself) ... to my astonishment, the nature of our discussions suddenly diverted to a much more personal conversation about his life. He never talks about his personal life, but at this moment in time I felt that he wanted to talk ... so we continued on, which led him to some striking realisations. He finished by saying, "How on earth did I manage to do that?" as he walked away ... What a result!

I hope you can agree ... results don't get much better than this! So, now it's your turn ...

What I'm Going to Focus on is:

1)
2)
3)

> To effectively communicate, we must
> realize that we are all different in the way
> we perceive the world and use this understanding
> as a guide to our communication with others.
> **~ Tony Robbins ~**

Chapter 5
Let's Peel Back The Onion on This!
What are you really about?

In life we do not attract what we want,
we attract who we are.
~ Moffat Machingura ~

Getting to Know Yourself at All Levels

Presupposition 7: We are more than our behaviour.

Our true potential is both unknown and unknowable, but can you *sense* just what you can achieve? In being drawn to reading this book, I imagine you have some sight of this, but the process of turning this sense into a reality is the sticking point. At the moment, you may well be out of sync with yourself. For example, at one level you may be wanting success, at another you may be anxious about being "out there," and at even another level there may be great value in spending time with your family, while at another you may yearn to make a difference in the education of children in Africa. The levels here clearly don't fit with each other. This misalignment leads you to feel that whatever level you are working in, nothing feels quite right or congruent.

The next two chapters are based around neurological levels (from NLP) as formulated by Robert Dilts and Todd Epstein. We are going to explore you within seven different hierarchical levels.

The levels I am referring to are:

1. The environment that you spend your time in.
2. Your behaviours.
3. The capabilities (or skills) that you have.
4. The beliefs you hold within you.
5. What you value.
6. Your identity.
7. Your vision and mission in life.

In understanding how you operate in each level you can recognise any misalignments, as in the example above, and then you can work from within the higher levels (beliefs, values, identity and vision) to have greater influence over your actions.

For example, if you wanted to create a change in the "procrastination of starting your own business," you would need to look at this from each level, with the knowledge that the upper levels will be the ones that permanently effect change. So if we look at the upper levels here, at a *belief* level, you may believe that "I'm not good enough"; at a *value* level, you may value family as well as success; at an *identity* level, you may describe yourself as "I am an administrator" rather than "I am an innovator"; and at a *visionary* level, you haven't even gone there yet! Once you have this knowledge, you gain greater understanding as to why you are procrastinating and you can begin to explore and work with each of these levels in greater detail.

When all seven levels become aligned, you will find yourself in the right place, at the right time, and associating with the right people; you seem to do the right things appropriate to your goal; you know you have all the necessary skills to achieve your goal; you know that your goal fits with your values and fits with the kind of person that you are and that the effect you are having on the world is a positive one. You are aligned. When the levels are aligned in this way, you will find energy, drive, passion, and enjoy what you are doing. The achievement of your goals in life becomes natural, and the journey, not the end result, becomes your "driver."

Exercise 10: Exploring Your Inner Levels - Environment, Behaviours, Capacity and Beliefs

Environment: This refers to everything "outside" of you. It's a chance to review how much responsibility you are taking for yourself.

Answer the following questions:

1.   Who do you spend time with at the moment?
2.   Where do you spend a lot of your time?
3.   If you keep spending time with these people and in these places, will you achieve the success you want, or do you need to change where you spend your time, and with whom you associate?

Behaviours: Circle what you feel best describes you.

How are you motivated?	Proactive - (You get on with it.) Do you like to simply make a start, and see what happens?	Reactive - (You think about it.) Do you have to think about it, research, and plan and then begin?
	Towards - (What you	Away From - (What

How are you motivated? (Cont'd)	want.) Do you choose what you are going to do, because you want something (e.g. money, success, being fit?)	you don't want, and what you want to avoid.) Do you choose what you are going to do because you want to prevent something (e.g. being poor, a failure, overweight, and unhealthy?)	
	Motivated by what is improving, and evolving.	Motivated by what is new, and change (your job, etc.)	
How do you assess how you are doing in situations?	Internally-based evaluation. (You evaluate according to your own standards.)	Externally-based evaluation. (You evaluate on what others think.)	
Do you ...?	Focus on people, experiences, relationships, and feelings.	Focus on tasks, systems, ideas, and objects.	
How do you approach a project?	Focus on detail, at the loss of the bigger picture. In a project, you are someone who plans schedules, calculates costs, and works out the practical steps. You can make things happen, but you can lose a sense of why you are doing something.	Dislikes detail. Focusing on the bigger picture. In a project, you focus on the outcome and then find sometimes that you haven't made a start, as the detail is less interesting.	
Most	Independent – working	Independent – but with	Co-operative – you like being a

productive when?	alone.	others around.	part of a team.
How you view yourself/others/relationships. *I'm ok/you're ok.* Do you see everyone as equal and valuable? You listen to them and consider their views, as well as your own?			
I'm ok/you're not ok. Do you always think you are right, or your idea is the best?			
I'm not ok/you're okay. Do you think other people always have the better ideas; live better lives, are more together, and confident, etc.?			
I'm not ok/you're not ok. Do you see no one as really ok? You aren't, and neither are they.			

Describe yourself using the above examples and then highlight the benefits and limitations in being this way, for your future success.

Ask yourself if, and how, you would benefit from being different.

When I learned about the above patterns of behaviour, I realised that I missed the bigger picture as I was *so* hung up on details (the perfectionist side of me) which very much held me back. In getting immersed in what I was doing on my own, I missed the input of others, and also the sharing of ideas, that's so helpful for an auditory person, and for business success. In formulating and practicing the miracle scenario (in Chapter 3), the values and vision exercise (in Chapter 6) and the well-formed outcome (in Chapter 7), I began to embody the bigger picture and open out to the world, and people, sharing my thoughts, and hearing feedback on them. It makes life so much easier, and more enjoyable, having others really there with you, and personally being able to hold the bigger picture.

In business, from my experience, I believe there is a need to have the ability to flow comfortably between being proactive and reactive, detail and whole driven. Being a "towards" person allows the focus to be on what you want, rather than what you don't want, which means you attract something very different. Setting your own standards saves the need to wait for approval from others, for which you may be waiting a long time! Working independently and yet, co-operatively – interdependently - will give you the advantages of both approaches.

Also in being aware of, and appreciating how other people operate in this way, you can work within their world for a better outcome for all.

For example … In business, knowing when someone is externally influenced helps you to know that they will be more likely to do as you ask them, without many questions – more so than someone who is internally influenced. They will insist more on what *they* want!

If you are selling something to these two differently processing types of people, the first person you would *suggest* the "best product" to, and the second person you would ask what *they* thought first, and offer possible "best" products that resonate with their way of thinking, giving them options from which they can choose. If someone is an "away from" kind of person, then you can let them know how the product will prevent them from experiencing something "negative", but if they are a "towards" person, you will need to pitch your sale at what they will gain, if they buy into your product.

Imagine yourself with the different ways and approaches of being that will help you gain your desired success. What is it like?

Capabilities: This is about acknowledging what you do. Can you build rapport instantly? Can you make quick balanced decisions?

Can you solve an IT problem easily? Are you good at diffusing a heated discussion?

1.   What skills do you have?

2.   What skills can you draw on to achieve success?

3.   What skills will you need to acquire to make your goals and dreams a reality?

4.   How can you acquire these skills?

Beliefs:

In the words of the famous author, Napoleon Hill (1975), "What the mind can conceive and believe, it can achieve." If you believe you can be successful or if you believe you can't, that is what you will work towards.

O'Connor and Seymour (2003), in *Introducing NLP: Neuro Linguistic Programming*, offer a clear definition of beliefs. They write that beliefs are, "the generalisations we make about ourselves, others and the world and our operating principles in it. Beliefs are self-fulfilling prophecies that influence all our behaviours." (pg. 53)

Our beliefs are emotionally held opinions and are how we make sense and meaning of the world, and what we live by. There are three types of beliefs. Beliefs about who we are, *our identity* (e.g. I am clumsy, or I'm not good enough), about *the world* (e.g. "Life is hard", or, "There is plenty for everyone"), and about *others* (e.g. "Men are X", or "Women are Y"). They are views, not universal truths, that are generalisations, created from learned childhood messages and experiences.

As children we make meaning or sense of the things we experience, in an effort to keep us safe in our world as we grow up. We form these into generalisations, or personal truths, and these are absorbed and become beliefs. If I get bitten by a dog at the age of five, say, I might translate the meaning from this into *all dogs are dangerous.* Beliefs will be formed from our home life, from school and from society, or even from films, and news programmes we may have watched at the time. For example, I worked with someone who always felt unsafe, thus was anxious most of the time. As a child she can clearly remember, at the age of six, creating a belief that "The world is unsafe," from repeatedly seeing on television news bulletins, at the time reporting about Peter Sutcliffe - (the infamous Yorkshire Ripper).

I call our set of beliefs, our "rule book of life." We each open a book when we are born, our own personal book. From then on we form our story, we write the pages, and make rules about life and ourselves based on what we see, hear, feel, smell and taste, so that we can find our way in life. After about seven or eight years of age, the rules have pretty much been formed, confirmed and set. The language for the rules may become a little more sophisticated as we mature, such as "I self-sabotage," but the belief is still grounded in childlike meanings, and reactions. "I self-sabotage," may have started out as, "I always get it wrong," or, "I never get it right," or, "I always mess up."

Unless we take the time to explore our rulebook, we'll never become fully aware of what's in it, and how it's influencing our lives. Guaranteed, beliefs will be what we create, and what will hinder us (if they are limiting beliefs – or even unrealistic beliefs). They will stop us being our real selves.

If you are wondering why you struggle when making a presentation, when you know your subject material inside out, and are fully prepared, then there's a limiting belief, in operation. It may be a belief that you are stupid, or that you always mess up, or you will never be good enough, or that people will laugh at you. It will be unique to you and will need to be uncovered, and worked through, if you are to change your reactions.

We all act from our beliefs. If I believe that women are weak, then weakness is what I will look for, what I will notice, what I'll attract, and what I will create. I may try to be strong to prove that I am *not* weak (sounds familiar!), or I may surround myself with strong people, so that I *do* look weak, thus unsurprisingly confirming that I am weak. If I believe that I always make mistakes, then I will either make mistakes by the bucket load, to prove myself right, or I will become a perfectionist, trying to prove my belief wrong. However, I will never completely convince myself that the belief is not true.

This is because beliefs are based on a child's *meaning making* framework, and so are incredibly resistant to adult logic. We can often clearly see, logically, that a belief doesn't make sense, but the sense that it's true, won't go away. Someone may have a belief that they are a failure, yet, in their life, they have never failed at anything! They have passed their educational exams, driving test and got every job they ever applied for, yet they still believe, and feel, that they are a failure! How is this so? - Adult logic (let's call it evidence) vs. childlike *felt sense* of being a failure. Feelings will win hands down, every time!

What do you need to do about your limiting beliefs?

Firstly, recognise what your beliefs are and how they are working for you ... Let's do that now.

The following are ways of immersing yourself into becoming aware of your beliefs. They are to get you thinking and feeling at this deeper level. Sit with each part of the following, and write down what comes to mind. I have given you some examples, to help you get started:

1) Recognise your limiting beliefs by completing the sentences below. Give your own one-word answers, similar to the examples given. Give five answers, for each of the following.

These are *identity* beliefs:

I am ...
tough ... bad ... thoughtful ... stupid?

I cannot be successful because ...
I'm afraid ... I'll get it wrong ... I might shine?

These are *world* beliefs:

Life is ...
easy ... hard ... cruel ... full of surprises?

Money is ...
hard to come by ... wrong ... happiness?

Business is ...
cut and thrust ... exciting ... unpredictable?

These are *other people* beliefs:

People are ...
difficult ... untrustworthy ... kind

Bosses are ...
manipulative ... mean ... selfless

Do any of the above operate as beliefs that are *really* driving you, in your work? If so ... how?

So ... if you believe that money is hard to come by, have you financially struggled and had to work hard for it, or have you found a way to earn a lot of money easily, to try and prove this belief wrong?

2) Think back to some of the regular sayings or phrases that were conveyed to you as a child. These will also have become beliefs, in some shape or form.

For example, things that were innocently said to me as a child, and which formed into beliefs were "What will the neighbours think?" and, "Children should be seen and not heard." These became a rule about, "Keep myself to myself," which meant early on in my adult life I was a very private person. People didn't know much about me and I never talked about how I felt, or what was happening in my life.

Others included, "Hard work never hurt anyone," and, "You only get out what you put in." Thus, my rule became, "work hard," as if it were a command! And so I did! Of course, as an adult, one needs to work hard at the right thing, and in the right way! It took me a long time to realise that one.

3) How do you feel about money? Money, and success, *do* go together. So, let's explore beliefs that are there for you. Imagine walking into a very luxurious hotel, or restaurant, and ordering a top quality glass of champagne, before you've even looked at the price list. How is this? What thoughts and feelings come up for you?

Your reactions will give you an indication as to how you feel about money. If it's uncomfortable then there is a belief, or a set of beliefs, that will be operating, which may well be holding you back. Write your beliefs down about money, and about your relationship with money.

4) You may have found the above easy, or you may be struggling to find some of your beliefs. However you are experiencing it, let's continue and read the limiting beliefs examples below, and circle those that resonate within you. You will likely circle between five and ten.

Limiting Beliefs examples:

I don't count.
I'm not important.
I'm unlovable.
I'm not good enough.
It's all my fault.
I'm bad.
I can never be safe.
I have no control.
I cannot trust myself.
I can't be angry.
People will hurt me.
I can't be known.
I don't deserve happiness.
I ruin everything.
I'm stupid.
I can't succeed.
I'll never be anything.
I'll never amount to much.
I'll always be on the outside.
I don't deserve.
I'm not normal.
I am responsible for others.
I must rescue/protect others.
I must please others.
I must be in control.
I am ugly/unattractive.
I'm in the way.

I'm useless.
I will always be let down.
I'm a disappointment.
I'm not wanted.
I am powerful.
I'm a failure.
I'm not capable.
I will always be alone.
I'm childish.
I'm pathetic.
I'm out of control.
I'm not worth noticing.
My feelings aren't worth anything.
I can't cope.
My opinion is worthless.
I am wrong.
I can't speak up.
Life is pointless.
Life is hard.
There is no safety.
Money is evil.
More is better.
People can't be trusted.
Get them before they get me.
People are either good or bad.
Others will betray me.
Control others.

5) Now look at what you have written, from the above exercises 1 to 4, and draw up a list of the limiting beliefs that you feel influence your success. Decide on about five of them.

6) Now complete the table below and give each limiting belief a mark out of ten, in line with how strongly you believe it to be true. Get immersed into exploring where you learned the belief, and how it works for you now.

This is something similar to what I completed, when I started out on my journey of self-discovery.

Limiting Belief	
I'm a nuisance (9)	**Where I learned this** I was always told not to be a nuisance, so I therefore concluded that I must be a nuisance, and that clearly was a bad thing.
	How I live by it now I didn't ask people for help when I should have done, as I didn't want to be a nuisance, and asking for help meant I was being a nuisance.
	Is it helpful or limiting? Not helpful in business, or life, as I shut myself off from people, and from tapping into others' potential and talents, and had to work very hard!
I'm not intelligent (8)	**Where I learned this** I failed to get into grammar school, and always seemed to have to work harder than everyone else to get the grades. Now looking back I wonder if the "Work hard" belief was operating as well here.

I'm not intelligent (Cont'd) (8)	**How I live by it now** I constantly achieved academically, to try and prove this wrong, never quite getting there. It was exhausting!
	Is it helpful or limiting? It pushed me to achieve, work hard at academic writing, although I struggled to feel good enough. I have read many books, and know a lot of information. *But,* it halted me from being myself, and thinking for myself. I only had other people's opinions.
Life is unpredictable (10)	**Where I learned this** This is a universal truth, which means a common truth for us all. A fact of life. Life *is* unpredictable. We can never quite know what is around the corner. However, for me, having been in a life threatening car accident, from which my life changed completely, "Life is unpredictable," was held within me in a catastrophic and life threatening way.
	How I live by it now Safety and risk, limiting behaviours. Saving money for an emergency, although not knowing what would constitute an emergency. I had a safe job as a teacher and worked tirelessly to always "clear the decks," because you never knew what was around the corner.

	Is it helpful or limiting? This was very limiting. Exhausting at times and kept me living an everyday life, scared of change.

7) Now look at these, as if your best friend was telling you these beliefs were true for them. What would you say to them? Challenge them (and so yourself), as to why they are *not* true.

For example, I would tell my best friend, that, "If someone asked me for help, I would not consider they were a nuisance. I would *expect* them to ask me, as it's a really good feeling to help someone. If that is how I would expect someone else to be, then I have to take it on for myself. If you tell me you have a first degree, a further master's degree, had written academic papers and books, clearly you are intelligent, right? Life can be unpredictable, yes, but that is life, and what makes it challenging and fulfilling. Unpredictable can be traumatic, but usually it isn't; it's part of being human, and being in the world. Most of the time, things can be managed, and worked through, whatever has happened."

Sit with some of this logic for a while, keep reading how these beliefs were formed when you were a child, and consider the childlike qualities they have, the childlike felt sense and the child like reasoning. Are the beliefs really true for you as an adult, now?

8) Re-thinking and re-framing

These beliefs may be limiting, but they can also be turned into an asset, as long as they are re-framed into something genuinely more productive, and resourceful. Then you can be purposefully mindful of when they are operating un-resourcefully, and when they are resourceful. This will give you choices, and options.

Here's how you do it:

Belief	Positives from this
	This has enabled me to be incredibly resourceful, work productively and independently. I like the fact that I have this.
I'm a nuisance	**Changing self-perception: re-thinking and re-framing** **I'm self sufficient** *but* I need to be mindful that others like to help, and we will both benefit from this.
Belief	**Positives from this**
I'm not intelligent	This has pushed me to academically achieve doctoral degree-level study, where I have met many great people, and studied many fascinating ideas. From here I have learned how different we all are, regarding our writing, thinking and understanding. It has pushed me to explore what I mean by "intelligent," and work out just what I want, and who I am. A work in progress, then!

	Changing self-perception: re-thinking and re-framing
I'm not intelligent (Cont'd)	*This is simple …* **I am intelligent** I don't feel I am an academic (which is another limiting belief in some way), but I am happy not to consider myself as one.
Belief	**Positives from this**
Life is unpredictable	If I can survive the car crash, then I can pretty much get through anything. I know that whatever happens I will somehow find my way through. I will be able to make the decisions I need to. **Changing self-perception: re-thinking and re-framing** **Life is uncertain.** That's what makes it exciting.

9) Keep working on these. Look specifically at the ones that are preventing your success. If they are frustratingly keeping you where you are, then in uncovering them you can do something with them. Begin to own a more accurate perspective of yourself, life and other people. It can be exciting!

For me - I imagined myself as self-sufficient *and* able to ask for help and share with others, aware that I am an intelligent human being and excited by life, and what could be around the corner. When I practiced this, it felt like I was growing up, maturing in some way.

Exploring beliefs can be liberating. Just by knowing what is driving your actions and where they are coming from, can in itself set you free from them. Take a few moments now to think about just what you want to focus on, and then write them down.

What I'm Going to Focus on is:

1)
2)
3)

Incredible change happens in your life when you decide to take control of what you do have power over, instead of craving control over what you don't.
~ Steve Maraboli ~

Chapter 6
Let's Take it to The Next Level
A Woman of Value!

Your conscious beliefs are what you think you believe.
Your subconscious beliefs and deepest convictions are what
you really believe.
~ Dr Susan Shumsky ~

Exercise 11: Exploring your inner levels -
Values, Identity, Vision, and Mission.

Values:

Values are what really matter to us. They are the glue that holds our reality together. They are what determine our priorities, what motivates us, and they guide how we evaluate what we and others do, and have done. Values are our essential compass in life.

If I value adventure, then I will be drawn to look for and create opportunities in my life that give me this. I will assess what's happening in my life, and how content I am by how much adventure I perceive or experience there to be in it. If I value friendships, then I will look to create opportunities for friendships to flourish, and will spend energy and create time to be with friends, which will take precedence over, say my work life.

When the things that we do and the way we behave match our values, then we feel content. When what we are doing in life doesn't align with our values, we will likely feel unsatisfied, restless, unhappy and unmotivated. If we don't listen to this and do something to change it, we may well create symptoms that draw our attention to the fact that we are not happy. We might experience anxieties, develop headaches, begin to overeat or drink, or feel depressed, for example.

If I value adventure, thus join the fire service, police force or armed services, going out on the "front line", only to find that I get injured, and have to be moved to office-based work, I will very soon feel unsettled. If I value family life and find that I am working a seventy-hour week, then I will feel unhappy and in conflict with this imbalance. Whilst many successful people work long hours, there is something to be said for gaining a level of congruent balance in life, between our divided passions. It's about aligning our values, and giving them space.

Getting to know your values will help you in decision making, and with inner conflicts. You will be able to answer more honestly, and with a greater truth, questions like, "Should I start my own business?", "Should I take that promotion?", "Should I compromise, or stand firm with this situation?" It will help you realise why things aren't happening for you, and why opportunities are not presenting themselves to you.

Here are some explorations to help you find out what you value.

Defining your values: Explore the following, and write down what comes to mind.

1) Identify times when you have really felt alive, or when you feel alive in the present.
2) Identify times when you have felt so immersed in something, that time just flies by.
3) Identify when you feel at your most "natural."
4) What family values were held, when you were growing up?

Now determine your values based on what you have written above and answer the question ... "What is really important to me in my life?"

If you feel alive and immersed when talking to people, and finding out about what's happened to them, and helping them solve problems and get what's rightfully theirs, you may hold values of fairness and justice.

5) Now use the list of values below, and mark those that mean something to you. It's really important that you find exactly the right word that fits for you. Serenity is different from tranquillity, for example. There should be a deeper "feeling sense" when you find one of your values. A "yes, that's the one," type of experience, is what I mean.

List of Values

Abundance	Cooperation	Growth
Acceptance	Courage	Happiness
Accomplishment	Creativity	Harmony
Accountability	Credibility	Health
Accuracy	Curiosity	Honesty
Achievement	Education	Humility
Adaptability	Effectiveness	Humour
Adventure	Efficiency	Intimacy
Affection	Empathy	Intuition
Altruism	Endurance	Inventiveness
Ambition	Energy	Imagination
Appreciation	Equality	Independence

Approachability	Ethics	Individuality
Approval	Excellence	Insightfulness
Art	Fairness	Inspiration
Assertiveness	Faith	Integrity
Attractiveness	Fame	Intellect
Balance	Family	Serenity
Beauty	Fashion	Sharing
Belonging	Fitness	Strength
Calmness	Focus	Success
Capability	Freedom	Support
Certainty	Friendship	Teaching
Challenge	Dependability	Teamwork
Change	Determination	Thoroughness
Comfort	Devotion	Thoughtfulness
Commitment	Dignity	Tidiness
Community	Diligence	Tranquillity
Compassion	Directness	Trust
Competence	Discipline	Truth
Competition	Discretion	Understanding
Confidence	Diversity	Uniqueness
Conformity	Duty	Variety
Congruency	Drive	Vision
Consistency	Enjoyment	Vitality
Contentment	Enthusiasm	Wealth
Control	Generosity	Winning

6) Now choose your top ten values, from all those you have listed, in questions 1 to 5. To help, you can imagine scenarios to check out what you would choose to do in situations that highlight the values. For example, what would you rather do ... read this book (learning) or go out with friends (friendship)? This will help identify which values are more important than others, in this case learning or friendship. You of course may value both learning and friendship in the same way, but when push comes to shove, one will take precedence.

Here is an important point! You are *not* your values, so if they are not working for you – start working for them. When you become aware that you are not living to your potential, your possibilities, when you are frustrated with yourself because you are not moving through life towards something fulfilling and energising, then your work is not in line with your values.

7) Take a look at your list of ten values, and consider where you developed them, and if they are values that will help you move forward, in your success. Look at the table below and explore your values in the same way.

Here are some examples:

Value	
Perfection	**What are they based on?** Learning that making a mistake got you into trouble.
	How does this value help me in life now? As a policy maker in my company, it has meant that I am able to draw up contracts that are pretty "watertight." Letters that are sent out are impressive, as they are perfect!
	How does this value limit me in life now? Everything takes too long to do, and I have a lot of trouble getting on with people, as I am constantly asking them to re-do things.

Value	What are they based on?
	My parents believed that you could do anything that you want; as long as you put your mind to it and that you should see things through to the bitter end. Also that you should "go for broke" and achieve.
Drive	**How does this value help me in life now?**
	I will have a go at anything, and am focused to complete any task that I am given. I will work as long as it takes.
	How does this value limit me in life now?
	I don't always look after myself properly, as I am so caught up in the drive to get things done. Sometimes my body becomes so exhausted that I then become ill and have to take time off work.

Now choose the top 5 values that make the biggest impact on you.

List your values in order of priority:

1)

2)

3)

4)

5)

Do your values fit with your success path now, or what you want to do in the future?

Do you need to consider other values, or put certain values higher up in order of priority, if you are to be successful?

Identity:

I often hear phrases such as, "That just wasn't me!" or, "I feel the real me is trapped inside, trying to get out," or, "I don't know what came over me." All these statements are statements about you at an *identity* level. The ones that look to answer, "Who am I?" and, "Who is the real me?"

The "Who am I?" Exercise

This exercise develops your self-awareness, and brings your attention sharply to where you are at, within yourself. I urge you to do this at regular intervals to "check in" with your self-perception at any given time. I purposely ask this of myself, around twice per year.

Your answers are whatever comes from within you. They represent aspects of you, and your relationship with the world. You are looking to explore beneath the layers that you have, and tap into who you really are. This is your inner code. Consider how, "I work in business," is very different to, "I am a business woman," and what this will mean for someone.

Sit quietly for a few moments, and explore within you the question "Who am I?" Don't rush, just take your time.

Now complete the following sentences. Each answer *must* be different to the last.

1) I am ...
2) I am ...
3) I am ...
4) I am ...
5) I am ...
6) I am ...
7) I am ...
8) I am ...
9) I am ...
10) I am ...

What have you discovered as you wrote your list? Did you go deeper with your answers, as you approached your tenth, "I am ..."?

Now look at the categories below and see where your answers fit. There are no right or wrong answers, as you are revealing how you experience and perceive yourself, at this very moment in time.

Physical self-descriptors – Your physical qualities, E.g. I am 47, I am female, I am 5 feet 6 inches tall.

Social self-descriptors – Relationships and qualities that come from social standards, E.g. I am a daughter, I am English, I am a therapist, I am a tennis fan, I am a business woman.

Psychological self-descriptors – Psychological qualities that are not socially defined, E.g. I am passionate, I am focused, I am logical.

> What does this say about how you define yourself? Do you use a role (daughter, teacher, wife) or descriptive facts (age, height, etc.) or, from a more social or psychological stance?

> Do you describe yourself as a more positive or negative person?

Do you experience your list as assets and strengths, or limitations and restrictions?

Would you like to be able to change any of them?

Now let's focus in on who are you, as a woman professionally. Do the same "Who am I?" exercise, only this time ask, "Who am I at work?" or, "Who am I professionally?"

Complete the following sentences. Remember, each answer *must* be different to the last.

1) I am
2) I am …
3) I am …
4) I am …
5) I am …
6) I am …
7) I am …
8) I am …
9) I am …
10) I am …

What have you discovered? Is there alignment between "Who am I?" and "Who am I professionally?"

Begin to merge the two lists so that you, and you as a professional, become one and the same. Become congruent and genuinely you, for as much of the time as you can.

Your vision and mission in life

This isn't something that we always give ourselves time to think about. However, as the author, and success coach, Steven Covey (2004) writes, in *The Seven Habits of Highly Effective People*, formulating and writing down our mission in life, is crucial for our success. I advise you to give this some thought and put the words down on paper.

Here are four questions to help you work on your mission statement:

1) What would you regret not fully doing, being or having in your life?
2) If you could get a message across to a large group of people, who would those people be? And what would your message be?
3) Imagine you are nearing the end of your life (you have reached a ripe old age) and you are assessing and evaluating all that you have done, lived and achieved. What is it that you want to be able to say? I slept a lot? ... I watched some great TV? I could have worked harder? I made a difference? I learned compassion and humility? I experienced many different things? I helped change the face of therapy? (That's one of mine.)
4) What eulogy would you want someone to read about you? In fact, let's write your very own eulogy now! Write it now. What are you going to say?

A personal mission statement consists of three parts:

- What do I want to do?
- Who do I want to help?
- What value will I create?

Take some time now to answer these questions. Be really true to yourself here. Find meaning and purpose, have a vision, and hold it strong in your mind at all times.

Find your calling (because we all have one), and write it down in a paragraph.

Let's put the last two chapters all together and see where you are. Complete the following and see how they match or mismatch.

Level – *Environment*	
You!	**Alignment?**
I spend a lot of my time with … I spend a lot of my time at/in …	Will this help me to live the life I dream of and fulfil my potential? (yes/no)
Level – *Behaviours*	
You!	**Alignment?**
My habits are … (circle the one that fits) I am proactive/reactive. I am towards/away from. Internal-based evaluation/external-based evaluation. I like things to evolve/I like doing new things. I am a detail/bigger picture person. I like to work alone/with others/with others around. I'm ok/you're okay, I'm ok/you're not okay, I'm not ok/you're okay, I'm not ok/you're not okay	Will these help me to live the life I dream of and fulfil my potential? (yes/no)

Level – *Capabilities*	
You!	**Alignment?**
The skills I have are … The skills I would like to acquire are …	Will these help me to live the life I dream of and fulfil my potential? (yes/no)

Level – *Beliefs*	
You!	**Alignment?**
My top 5 beliefs are …. 1) 2) 3) 4) 5)	Will these help me to live the life I dream of and fulfil my potential? (yes/no)

Level – *Values*	
You!	**Alignment?**
What I value most is … 1) 2) 3) 4) 5)	Will these help me to live the life I dream of and fulfil my potential? (yes/no)

Level – *Identity*	
You!	**Alignment?**
1) I am … 2) I am …	Will these help me to live the life I dream of and fulfil my

3) I am … 4) I am … 5) I am …	potential? (yes/no)
Level – *Vision/Mission*	
You!	**Alignment?**
What I want to do is … I want to be … I want to help …. The result will be ….	How aligned am I?

There has been a great deal of personal exploration in these chapters, so take your time and go back to the levels where you feel you would like things to be different, and consider what you can begin to do differently … even if it's something small.

Now let's update and focus on where you're heading!

What I am going to focus on is:

1)

2)

3)

Every great dream begins with a dreamer. Always remember, you have within you the strength, the patience, and the passion to reach for the stars to change the world.
~ Harriet Tubman ~

Chapter 7
This is Your Deliverable – Going Viral!
What's after my goals?

I have learned over the years that when one's mind is made up, this diminishes fear; knowing what must be done does away with fear.
~ Rosa Parks ~

Your Aspirations

Knowing what you want is important. Knowing what that will give you is crucial, and knowing what you will do *next* is central if the mind is going to fully engage in seeking to achieve your goals. It's being able to concisely answer … "If I gain that promotion, what will that give me, and where will it take me next?" It has to be really worth it for you to hold it, and embody it, effortlessly.

So ... What *will* being a successful woman do for you, in the grand scheme of your life? What will it give you? Once this is completely and firmly in place, and you are aligned with it, then *your* glass ceiling will no longer exist. You will be free to be all you can be.

Presupposition 8: As response-able people, we can run our own brain and control our results.

Let's take a look at how you hold your goals, the journey in achieving them, and what happens when you get there, so you can fully understand how things have been up until now.

Exercise 12: Your Aspirations

Find a quiet place and take yourself through a basic relaxation process. Then read the following visualisation, pausing to imagine what I will be suggesting to you. Just allow things to naturally unfold, and write down what comes into your mind.

Imagine yourself in a beautiful place in the countryside, like a field or meadow. You may have been there before, or it may be an imaginary place; it really doesn't matter. There is nobody else around to bother you, and all is peaceful and calm. Make this place just right, to create an inner feeling of peace and tranquillity. Notice if it's sunny, if there are any sounds around you, if there are flowers, trees or shrubs. Wander around and enjoy this place for a while, immersing yourself in the peace, calmness and quiet. Then, you notice a path leading off into the distance, and you begin to walk along it ... And ...

1) Ahead of you, in the distance, you see a mountain ... what does it look like? What thoughts do you have as you look at the mountain?

2) Walk towards the mountain and stand at the bottom, and look up. What is it like? Can you see the top? Again, what are you thinking about as you look at the mountain, and how do you feel?

3) Now begin to climb the mountain. What is the terrain like? How is the experience for you in climbing the mountain? ... What makes you choose the path up the mountain that you have? How long does it take you to get to the top? Can you get to the top? Write down in detail what the journey up the mountain is like for you.

4) Place an obstacle in the way. All of a sudden, your path is blocked. How does this feel? Is it an object, perhaps a large boulder, or fallen tree, or a person? What do you do next?

5) You are now at the top. What is it like? How does it feel? What do you notice?

6) Now what would you like to do?

7) Just begin to take yourself down the mountain now and back into the field/meadow.

So how was that?

Now, let's make some sense and meaning of this journey up the mountain, taking it into deeper levels of how you actually hold your aspirations, goals and how you move towards them.

Begin to consider how the mountain (representing your goals), your journey up the mountain (the process of getting there), and what it was like at the top of the mountain (how it feels and what happens when you have actually reached your goal), mirrors how you are at the moment when working towards and achieving your goals.

·

Let me give you a few examples of what some women on my success programmes describe, and the meaning they took away from this process.

Jane went only halfway up the mountain before she couldn't be bothered to go any further. She sat down for a while, and then wanted to return to where she started. *When we explored it, she could recognise how she starts something, but then quickly loses interest, stops doing whatever it is, and goes back to how it always used to be, wondering when something different will occur.*

Rachel started at the bottom and before I even asked her to begin her journey to the top, had already got there! She was then waiting around, disappointed and looking for the next mountain to climb. *She recognised that she goes into projects like a "bull in a china shop," not worried about the process, but just getting to the end result as quick as possible. Once there, she is often disappointed and looks to do something else. The grass is always greener on the other side for her.*

Lisa found the steepness of the mountain really tough going. She needed to look for equipment that would help her. She needed to rest half way up, taking in the view. She was so tired she couldn't quite get there, running out of steam. She wanted to come down three quarters of the way up. *She talked about how her goals in life seemed so hard to achieve. She always felt she had never quite done anything in life as she always ran out of enthusiasm as she neared her goal and found herself drawn back to staying where she was at.*

Other people's examples described feeling very alone and isolated at the top of the mountain, everyone and everything so far away (holding achievement as a lonely place to be). When someone else got to the top, there were swirling dark clouds and they were terrified (being successful, linked to something terrifying happening.) Another found that at the top it was disappointing and just a small peak, with nowhere to stand. Others have been at a loss as to what to do, once they were at the top. One person floated to the top of the mountain and realised that actually in life at that time, she didn't feel grounded. All different experiences, and all meaningful, in how reaching goals and aspirations are deeply held within these people.

What are you taking away from this guided imagery? What does it mean about you, and achieving your goals?

During this imagery, when I suggested you placed an obstacle on the path, what happened for you?

Examples of responses for this have been simply stopping and feeling unable to go on, looking around for a new path, or something that would help them to get around it, over or through it. How do you deal with challenges in life, and do they relate symbolically to your reaction to the obstacle on the path?

We can also use this visualisation to symbolically move forwards and make inner changes, and so I would like you to decide on a change in your imagery, that would symbolically change your goal, the journey or what is was like, when you got there.

For example ... if you raced to the top of the mountain, you could practice slowing the journey down, and taking in the views along the way. If you found it disappointing at the top, or felt at a loss of what to do next, you could imagine making the top of the mountain different or you could imagine standing at the top, taking some time to look around, to be aware of how it feels, and then ask yourself what you would really like to do now ... I mean *really* like to do. Then imagine you are doing it. Somebody I once worked with wanted to fly off the top of the mountain and enjoy the freedom and control this gave them. Why not? Great - let's see how it feels.

You could even begin to rehearse the journey that you would really like to have when ascending the mountain, symbolising the journey in life and movement towards the goals that you want. Don't forget to always include what you will do once you've got to the top. It's crucial to have in place the goal that comes *after* the goal. As Winston Churchill once famously said, "Plans are nothing; planning is everything"

Practice the visualisation and make some changes to it and see the difference it makes.

> Your goal should be out of
> reach but not out of sight.
> ~ *Anita DeFrantz* ~

The Well-Formed Outcome

Now you know how you hold your aspirations within you, and have begun to creatively make some changes, let's zoom in on the detail.

Exercise 13: The Well-Formed Outcome (WFO)

The well-formed outcome is a strategy for opening you up to just what it is that you want. It's the combination of the bigger picture and the specific details that, once created, becomes embedded, and embodied, within. It begins to programme you for achieving the goal that you want. It is one of the most powerful strategies within the NLP model.

Extensively written about by Robert Dilts, and exquisitely described and unpacked by Bodenhammer and Hall (2001) in *The User's Manual for the Brain*, the WFO offers an advanced way of breaking down the nuances of your goals, so that you can see where you want to go, what might be stopping you and what can help. The whole point of NLP is about getting specific, direct and clear as to what you want. The WFO helps you do just that.

So, let's do it now. Let's create your own unique WFO. As before, there are no right or wrong answers. The only rule is that you need to answer each question in turn. Don't move onto the next question until you are fully satisfied you have written what you need to say for each question. Read the questions, and complete the sentences one by one. If you have someone that you can talk this through with, then this will really help develop things further.

The WFO Process

1. What do you want from being successful?
I want ...

2. What does having success do for you?
Having success will ...

3. How will you know when you have success?

Imagine that in three different situations.
    a. At work I ...
    b. Socially I ...
    c. In my relationships I ...

4. Imagine that has all happened. How do you think?

Imagine that in three different situations.
    a. At work I think ...
    b. Socially I think ...
    c. In my relationships I think ...

5. Imagine that all this has actually happened. How do you feel?
I feel ....

6. Do you need help to maintain this way of being, or can you do it on your own?

I need …
I can …

7. When you have success, how do you experience this?

a. Where I experience success is …
b. When I experience success is …
c. With whom I experience success is …

8. When you're successful, is there anything negative about it which could have a detrimental impact on your life?

Being successful might be difficult because …

9. What would you need to be successful?

To be successful I need …

10. What could stop you achieving ultimate success?

The only thing that could stop me from achieving ultimate success is …

11. When you are successful, what positive benefits of staying the same might you lose?

Because I am now successful I may lose …

12. Is becoming successful worth the cost in money?

Yes / No

13. Is becoming successful worth the cost in time?

Yes / No

14. Does being successful agree with your sense of self? Does it align with your values and mission?

Yes / No

Bonus Number 3

Because this is such a crucial part of smashing your glass ceiling and guiding yourself to success, I am giving you a free demonstration of the well-formed outcome exercise, in action, which you can download and watch now. That way you can gain a clearer insight as to the detail you need to get down to. Simply go to www.SandraWestlandMedia.com and you will be able to download your copy absolutely free. Watch, learn and enjoy.

Keep revisiting the well-formed outcome exercise, and imagine yourself successful, and how you will be enjoying this success. How will you think, feel, and act? Begin to create and run different kinds of movies in your mind, showing different successful situations, so that you are taking this within, at all levels. Your unconscious mind has no sense of time, which is why past failures seem like they happened only yesterday, so in programming yourself for success, your deep inner mind, that most powerful force within you, will soon believe that you can achieve the heights you are programming it to achieve, which means you will then, very soon, make this a reality ... *your* reality!

Now ....

Take some action towards your goals. Do something. If you can't, at this stage, think of what specific action will bring your goals to fruition, then do something different anyway ... get your neurological pathways flexing their muscles, and forming new routes. It needn't be complex. Wear your watch on the other wrist, or go to a different restaurant. Make a commitment with yourself that from today, you will do something *each day* that you have never done before. It doesn't have to be huge. If you normally eat a tuna sandwich for lunch, then try cheese. If you always take the same route to work, try a different one. I'm going to say it again, because it's so powerful and so true – "If you always do what you've always done, you'll always get what you've always got." – so go for it!

Let's create action and momentum!

What I'm going to *do* is ...

1)
2)
3)

It's great having your bigger picture well and truly in place and well formed, but what about the little niggling behaviours, that can still hinder you and hold you up, simply making life difficult. Things like getting impatient with somebody, or feeling awkward when you are socialising, or speaking on the phone. These things can quickly be altered through learning some state changing techniques, so that they support the overall movement towards your ultimate success.

Do one thing every day that scares you.
~ Eleanor Roosevelt ~

Chapter 8
It's Just a Bad Day at The Office
How can I change my reactions to ...?

There are two ways of meeting difficulties.
You alter the difficulties or you alter yourself to meet
them.
~ *Phyllis Bottome* ~

Pre-supposition 9: *We already have the resources we need to get what we want.*

Now you have greater awareness as to how you work, and you have the bigger picture and are already doing some things differently, what is likely happening is that you are finding some old habits frustrating to break. "Old habits die hard," my mother used to say (another limiting belief I needed to shed). Maybe you are still getting tense when speaking to a potential customer, or you are getting stressed when the phone rings, or you're procrastinating about answering that email. Changes take time to embody before they become new habits.

Just think for a moment - when you have made a change in your kitchen cupboards or living room drawers, and moved things around, how often have you found yourself going to where you used to place the kitchen utensils or the magazines, before you remember you had moved them? I put a hand towel holder in the bathroom in a different place once, and for several months I *still* went to where the hand towel used to be, to dry my hands. I have read that it takes twenty-eight days to change a habit! It took much longer for me with a hand towel! I clearly like to evolve my changes, take my time to embody them as "me," and "mine." More scientific research has found that it was difficult to actually conclude how long changes take to sink in, depending very much on the individual and what they were trying to change. A habit is basically a set of neurological connections, so it's a complicated process to alter overnight. Research now suggests that it takes on average about sixty-six days to change a behaviour, and create a new habit. There's a challenge!

The moral of the story? Have patience with yourself!

However, this doesn't stop us from speeding things up a bit for you.

Sometimes in life things don't go as we planned, or we feel totally out of alignment with ourselves, or there are particular scenarios that we aren't handling in the way that we would like, or we can simply wake up in a bad mood, and then our day seems to go from bad to worse. I'm sure you can resonate with the saying, "I got out of the wrong side of the bed." All of these are states that we slip into, which are not helpful to us and which we can struggle to shake off. To operate at our fullest potential, we need to be in the state that enables us to get the results we want, be it chairing a meeting, fronting a presentation, answering the phone, or dealing with customers or clients. We need to be able to move into the most resourceful state that we can, for the job in hand. When things go wrong, we need to be able to pull ourselves out of the state that we've moved into, so that it doesn't impact the rest of our day, month, year, or the rest of our life!

States affect your capabilities. How well you perform is dependent on the state you are in at the time. So whatever it is that you are doing, ask yourself, "What state do I need to be in?" When things are not going well, or you have a habit you want to change, then ask yourself, "What state do I need to be in?" and then you need to be able to change to that state.

I have referred to "states" quite a lot here, so what do I mean? A state is a combination of your physiology, neurology, biochemistry and psychology that creates your subjective experience of yourself and the world at any given moment. We go through many states just in one day. I'm sure you can recognise a tired state, agitated state, annoyed state, or happy or relaxed state for example.

If we want to change our states, so that we are operating at our optimum performance, there is a need to change our internal focus, our physiology, neurology, biochemistry and psychology, and our inner self-talk.

Here's how we do it ...

a) To change your internal focus, you can use some effective NLP techniques. We'll look more deeply into these soon.
b) To change your physiology, you need to move, I mean *physically* move. This will shift different chemicals throughout your body, and thus will change your physiological make-up. Changing your posture, facial expression, walking, or stretching will all create a chemical change in your body and thus change your physiological state. So if you are becoming angry, anxious or panicky for

whatever reason, then move about. Try sitting, lying down, or walking - any way that is really different for you!

c) To change your self-talk, you need to make sure that it's positive and encouraging. It's not helpful to have a voice constantly telling you how useless you are, and pointing out all the mistakes you have supposedly made. Be a little nurturing in your-self talk. Encourage yourself, praise yourself, believe in yourself a little more. It's a much nicer experience than berating, criticising and damning yourself. Imagine you are talking to a young child - what would you say to them and how would you say it, to help them feel good about themselves, and achieve success?

Let's look at three techniques that NLP offers that can make those inner state changes happen, as and when you need to create them.

The three techniques we are going to explore are:

1) **The Resourceful Self Technique**
2) **The Anchoring Technique**
3) **The Swish Technique**

We are going to use these three methods to re-programme some of your current responses, so that doing things differently happens from the inside and effortlessly.

These techniques are three of the most powerful ones. There are an abundance of other techniques that can help you break the states that are linked with your unwanted and old responses, but these three really hit the spot. If you would like to read more about these techniques and master them, then take a look at *Thinking Therapeutically: Hypnotic Skills and Strategies Explored*, Westland and Barber (2011) – which you can get (with a free chapter) at www.ThinkingTherapeutically.com.

You see, you can't solve a problem or change behaviour from the same state of awareness that *created* it. You will never be able to stop eating chocolate if you remain in the chocolate eating state! If you simply try and change the behaviour, then you will be forcing will-power, where a huge amount of energy is then focused on what you *shouldn't* be doing, such as *not* eating chocolate. If you look to transform your state to a more resourceful one, then things will start to happen naturally.

Let's start by taking all that you have created in the miracle scenario and the well-formed outcome, and integrate everything into a detailed perception of you that has all the resources that you need, with the details that your mind can get hooked into and work with at all levels. You can step into this Resourceful Self whenever you need to change a state. You could even imagine her taking over the situation, as if you have become just a passenger, or a bystander in dealing with a situation.

Let's do it, and see how you get on.

Exercise 14: The Resourceful Self Technique

1) **Imagine yourself in your most resourceful state. This is the you that has every inner resource needed, to achieve all you could want.** Make this image as real as possible, noting what clothes, facial expression, mannerisms, voice tone, language and stance you have.

2) **Now explore what this you does when she is under stress at work. What does she do that makes her so resourceful in this situation?** Is she calm and patient? Is she assertive? Does she ask for help? Clearly, as you have *all* the resources you need, you can handle the situation well, can't you?

3) **How does this you handle making a mistake?** Does she shrug it off? Do you look to learn from it? Or does she apologise if she needs too?

4) **How is this you when a setback has occurred at work?** Again, remember this is not you now, but this is the you that already has all the inner resources to handle yourself in life as you want too. What happens?

5) **How does this you combine her personal and professional life, seamlessly?**

6) **How does this you socialise at work?**

   Rehearse each scenario (2 – 6) and make sure that it really feels right for you. Work at this so that you can imagine it, clearly and effortlessly.

7) **Now step into that you and imagine looking out through her eyes. Notice what it is like and the difference between how you are now, and how you will be in the future.** For example, do things move slower within you? Do you feel more grounded? Are there fewer worries? Are there limiting beliefs that are no longer there?

   Note that *you* have created this you, so this actually *is* who you really are; you just now have to acknowledge, and embrace it.

Practice this visualisation so that your mind can begin recognising it and can re-ignite it when needed and then soon she will become naturally the prominent you.

When I was learning to play the piano, I had to firstly listen to a piece of music played by someone else, and then hear it in my head. Afterwards I had to imagine me playing the notes perfectly, and then begin to practice the piece physically over and over again, until it became part of me. I could then sit down and simply play the piece without thinking about it. I could immerse myself in the meaning of the notes and the combination of the melody, and what it told me, so I could express it in my way. Neurologically, my brain had assigned neurons to the activity, and eventually created the relative circuit. This is what we want your resourceful self to recreate within you.

Exercise 15: The Anchoring Technique

Anchoring is one of the fundamental tools of NLP that helps you to increase confidence, enthusiasm, or whatever else you desire to achieve. What is an anchor? It is quite simply a stimulus-response situational mechanism. It is any sensory experience (stimulus) that, when repeated, creates the same response each time. Anchors operate in our lives constantly. Some are positive and some are not so positive.

Some examples are:

A positive visual anchor could be a photograph of one of the most relaxing holidays you have ever had. When you see the picture, it brings forward those very same feelings of relaxation and happiness.

A positive kinaesthetic anchor could be the experience of sitting in your chair at work, which takes you to a competent, confident state.

The sound of a certain piece of music can evoke either a certain nostalgic state or a very upbeat state. Do you ever play music in your car to make yourself feel better?

Smells are powerful anchors as well. A familiar perfume, a specific food smell, or the smell of coffee, can all elicit thoughts, feelings, and images from the past, taking us to a particular experience we've had, which changes the present state that we are in.

A negative anchor could be seeing the boardroom table at work, a sight that prompts feelings of anxiety. Or it might be the sound of somebody's voice, which elicits anger or frustration.

It's easy to *create* anchors for yourself, where you set up a purposeful stimulus-response pattern to create the state that you need, so that you can recreate the feeling that you want to experience, whenever you need to. Imagine what it would be like if you could, in any given moment, go from feeling anxious, to feeling confident and capable right in the middle of a stressful situation, within a split second.

Let's learn the technique of creating an anchor, so that when you experience a difficult situation, such as dealing with a work colleague or business client, who has a special talent for getting on your nerves, you can rely on your specially-created *calmness* anchor, and instantly feel a freedom from that tormenting and irritating scenario! This is how you do it …

1) **Identify the desired emotional state you want, e.g. confidence, calmness, enthusiasm, etc.** You need to define very specifically how you *want* to feel, not how you *don't* want to feel. For example, choosing to feel powerful and enthusiastic, rather than *not* wanting to feel anxious and irritable.

2) **Once you have selected the desired state, recall a particular time in your life when you felt that desired state.** Pick a powerful example. Look back into your past to recollect times when you had this desired state. The context is unimportant; what *is* important is remembering a few particularly strong experiences, and then selecting the most powerful one. The more pure and significant the experience

that you choose, the better. If you can't find one, then create one in your imagination of how that *would* be, had it been as powerful as you would have liked.

3) **Now create this state in your imagination by mentally transporting yourself back into that experience, as if it is happening in this very moment.** Notice what you see, hear what you are hearing, feel what you are feeling in this moment. Allow it to be *as if* it is happening, right now.

4) **Just as the state is about to peak in its intensity, make a fist with your hand and say a word or phrase that *captures* the feeling, while also visualizing an image that represents the state.** E.g. clench your left fist, as you softly but also confidently say to yourself, "calm," and, "relax" ... whilst you picture someone who represents calmness and relaxation for you, perhaps a Buddhist monk or a child giggling, or you can picture *yourself* in this state, in your most powerful form. Hold the state for a few moments, then release the anchor (your fist) and next break the state. Think about something completely different, and change your posture. Stand up; turn around 360 degrees or stretch. Move yourself so you change your physical state.

Now go through this process five more times, in order to build a resilient and well-formed anchor. This repetition is vital to the success of this technique.

5) **Test the anchor. Make the fist, say the words "calm," and, "relax," picture the person that represents calmness, and then check that you experience the desired state.** You will know that you have successfully anchored this resourceful state when you can access the desired state by making the fist, saying the words, imagining the person, and then *becoming* calm. If the desired state isn't strong enough, then choose a different experience that more precisely gives you

the appropriate state, and keep doing this, until you get the response you want.

Reinforce this technique periodically to make sure the anchor stays strong, and is effective when you need it.

Exercise 16: The Swish Technique

The Swish technique enables you to quickly disperse the *image* that you hold of the un-useful response or state, and *replace* this with a more useful, and resourceful state. This rapid and effective process re-programmes the current pattern of response, by instructing the brain, *"No … not that … this!"* When practiced enough, the old response becomes defunct, deleted, and subsequently forgotten, and the mind can only find the image that creates the response you want. You are training yourself to redirect your thinking and focus. This is pure NLP reprogramming, at its most powerful.

By using the Swish pattern in your own life, you will develop your ability to maintain resourceful states, manage your responses to stressful situations, and generate the behaviours you want.

The steps are as follows:

1) **Create an image of how you want to be in a current problematic situation. What state do you want?** Ask yourself, *"How do I want to be in this situation instead?"*
It is important that this image is of you, looking at yourself. Enhance the detail within the image and the quality of the picture, until the image is compelling for you.

2) **Create an image of what is happening just before you engage in the unwanted behaviour.** Ask yourself, *"What occurs just before this unwanted state begins?"*
Find the trigger for the unwanted state. Is it hearing the voice of the person, seeing them walking towards you, the

ringing of the phone or the sound of an email coming into your mailbox, for example?

This time, you want to be looking out through your own eyes immediately *before* you engage in the unwanted behaviour.

3) **As in *figure 8.1* below, put the replacement image: how you *want to be* in the corner of the unwanted image: how it is now just before you go into the unwanted state.**

Imagine a small postage-stamp sized version of your replacement picture in the top corner of the unwanted picture.

Figure 8.1

4) **Now ... switch the two images.**

Make both images change simultaneously. So, make the unwanted image smaller and shooting off into the top right hand corner, whilst at the same time, the positive replacement image become larger and closer. Imagine a "swish" sound as you swap the images over.

SWISH *This Picture* → to *This Picture*

5) **Now ... Clear your mind. Think of something entirely different for a moment, to move you out of this state.**

6) **Next, and most importantly, you need to repeat this same process for a total of 7 times.**

After each Swish round, clear your mind as in Step 5. It is crucial to the success of the Swish process to clear your mind or turn your attention outside, before you do the next round.

Feedback: How did you find these three techniques? Did you prefer one technique more than the others? If so, what made the difference for you?

All of these reprogramming techniques require practice, so every day, as you get up in the morning, or while you are perhaps on the train going to work, or at lunchtime, do your mental muscle exercises! The results will be worth it, and you will notice the changes rapidly taking place.

You can use these techniques in any situation where you want to change your reactions and responses. This is how you can reprogram yourself and your behaviours in a very specific way, and make a monumental difference to how you experience life.

Nothing will work unless you do.
~ Maya Angelou ~

Chapter 9
At the end of the day, just be extraordinary

Overcome the notion that you must be regular.
It robs you of the chance to be extraordinary.
~ Uta Hagen ~

We are now at the end of the Success programme. There is still so much more that we could explore and countless skills and techniques you could learn, but this book has been about stepping into and creating your journey and making that all important start. In getting to the end of this book you really have done that. I hope you can feel proud. Well done. You have already begun to create a new future with endless possibilities.

At this stage, I would love to know how you have got on with the exercise workouts and the techniques that you have learned. Go now to my reader feedback and comments page at www.SmashingYourGlassCeilingFeedback.com and take a few moments to leave me some feedback on what's changing for you, and how you've found the techniques working for you specifically. From the feedback page you can then also find out about others' experiences, and get the additional bonus of learning from those who have experienced them also, and how they have adapted these techniques, as well as other ways of discovering your potential so you can get really creative, and do the same.

Being Extraordinary

Being a woman *is* extraordinary, and I am proud to be one. I hope this book has taken you to this place also and that you will somehow be inspired by what you have learned. When you do this, you instantly make a difference, and become extraordinary and visionary yourself, in that one simple step.

A visionary will always see the bigger picture, thinking new for themselves and others. They will be able to move beyond the ordinary and the "everyday," embracing possibilities, potential, freedom, passion and self-learning. This is you.

Keep being curious and keep learning. Re-assess where you are and check in with yourself regularly. And when you find a small glitch … re-read each chapter again, read something new or attend a workshop that will allow you the space for further exploration!

> Knowing yourself is the
> beginning of all wisdom.
> **~ Aristotle ~**

Bonus Number 4

I'm now going to offer you my final bonus. I'm inviting you to London to spend two whole days with me learning about hypnosis and NLP, for free! Yes, entirely free! I want to reserve you a place as a thank you for reading this book, and completing the exercises and workouts to move you into being an extraordinary woman. There's so much more to learn about the mind, and I am passionate about supporting as many people as possible to take charge of their lives. It's my own personal well-formed outcome if you like.

In our two days together, you will learn how to enhance your journey into success with the additional power of hypnosis, learning how this can propel your voyage into success even further. You will find out about the different states of hypnotic trance, brain states and frequencies and various ways of achieving the hypnotic trance and exploring the powerful use of suggestion, to access your deep inner mind.

Along with me is Tom Barber (author of *The Book on Back Pain: The Ultimate Guide to Permanent Relief* - _www.TheBookOnBackPain.co.uk_), and together we will explore how you can further use NLP, described by *Psychology Today* magazine as, "the most powerful vehicle for change in the 21st Century."

To get your ticket to attend these packed two days of certified training, for absolutely free, simply visit the information and booking page at www.FreeHypnosisAndNLPCourse.co.uk. There you will see when the next course is running, and can book your place immediately online.

The Ultimate Success Workshop

To experience the exercises and techniques along with other people in an experiential way makes a remarkable difference in how you understand and implement them at a deeper personal level. So many people who have done, for example, the well-formed outcome, on their own, and then completed this exercise with someone else listening and asking them probing questions (with guidance), have found that it takes their awareness of themselves, and who they are, to a much deeper and more profound level.

This is why I want to also tell you about my totally new **Ultimate Success Workshop**, which has been the culmination of my many years of education, therapeutic practice, teaching, coaching, and workshop experience. I have fine-tuned (and continue to do so) what really works for women in the path to success, and then formulated the best possible concentrated two-day intensive experience, for you to smash your glass ceiling, and be all you can be. I've launched my workshop for you to really take the time to go deeper into yourself, gaining the understanding you need, and to learn from a wealth of successful techniques that will not only move you forward, but propel you to a place you are just beginning to imagine. There is so much more than this book could ever cover, that will help you further become the woman that you really are. You can find out more about where your nearest venue is and book your very own Ultimate Success Workshop place at www.SmashingYourGlassCeiling.com.

I hope to see you there and I hope this book has transformed your relationship with yourself, so that you can now truly believe that smashing your glass ceiling is not only possible, but it is already happening.

If not now ... when?

Would you tell me, please, which way
I ought to go from here?
*That depends a good deal on where you
want to get to.*
~ Lewis Carroll, *Alice in Wonderland* ~

Resources

www.SmashingYourGlassCeiling.com – Order further copies of *Smashing the Glass Ceiling.*

www.UltimateWomensBootcamp.com – Join Sandra and others for two days of powerful, inspirational, life-changing and transformational change.

www.SmashingYourGlassCeilingFeedback.com – Leave Sandra feedback on how you have used her methods and join her social media sites to hear others stories of success.

www.SandraWestlandMedia.com – Get help and resources written about in this book.

www.ThinkingTherapeutically.com – Sandra Westland and Tom Barber's highly acclaimed book on hypnotherapy, NLP and imagery.

www.ContemporaryCollege.com – UK certified training in hypnosis, hypnotherapy, NLP, counselling and psychotherapy.

www.FreeHypnosisAndNLPCourse.co.uk – Your bonus free course in hypnosis and NLP skills.

www.WriteYourUltimateBook.com – Explore Raymond Aaron's amazing 10-10-10 program.

www.TheBookOnBackPain.co.uk – Tom Barber's book on getting the ultimate relief from pain.

www.SandraWestland.com – Sandra's personal therapy website.

References

Barber, T. and Westland, S. (2011) *Thinking Therapeutically: Hypnotic Skills and Strategies Explored*. Carmarthen: Crown House Publishing.

Bodenhamer, B. and Hall, M. (2000) *The User's Manual for the Brain: Volume 1*. Carmarthen: Crown House Publishing.

Brady, K. (2013) *Strong Women: The Truth About Getting to The Top*. London: HarperCollins Publishers Ltd.

Covey, S. (2004) *The Seven Habits of Highly Effective People*. London: Simon and Schuster.

Hill, N. (1975) *Think and Grow Rich*. NY: Fawcett Books.

Knight, S. (2009) *NLP at Work: The Essence of Excellence – (3rd Ed. - People Skills for Professionals)*. London: Nicholas Brealey Publishing.

O'Connor, J. and Seymour, J. (2003) *Introducing NLP: Neuro Linguistic Programming*. London: Thorsons.

Roddick, A. (2000) *Business as Unusual: The Journey of Anita Roddick and The Body Shop*. London: Thorsons.

Shambaugh, E. (2008) *It's Not a Glass Ceiling: It's a Sticky Floor*. NY: McGraw Hill.

Further Reading

NLP:

Agness, L. (2010) *Change Your Life With NLP: The Powerful Way to Make Life Better*. Harlow: Pearson Life.

Dweck, C. (2012) *Mindset: How You Can Fulfil Your Potential*. NY: Random House.

O'Connor, J. (2001) *NLP Workbook: A Practical Guide to Achieving the Results You Want*. London: Thorsons.

GAI:
Macbeth, J. (2002) *Sun Over Mountain: A Course in Creative Imagery*. Berkshire: Gateway.

Stewart, W. (1995) *Imagery and Symbolism in Counselling*. London: Jessica Kingsley.

Mind-Body Connection:
Brizendine, J. (2008) *The Female Brain*. London: Bantam Press.

Damasio, A. (2000) *The Feeling Of What Happens: Body, Emotion and the Making of Consciousness*. London: Vintage.

Gallagher, S. (2006) *How the Body Shapes the Mind*. Oxford: Oxford University Press.

Existential Philosophy/Practice:
Adams, M. (2013) *A Concise Introduction to Existential Counselling*. London: Sage Publications.

Arnold-Baker, C. and Van Deurzen, E. (2005) *Existential Perspectives on Human Issues: A Handbook for Therapeutic Practice*. Hampshire: Palgrave MacMillan.

Index

be all you can be

TRAINING IN

HYPNOTHERAPY
•
PSYCHOTHERAPY
•
COUNSELLING
•
NLP

www.ContemporaryCollege.com

85086101R00083

Made in the USA
Lexington, KY
29 March 2018